N/A

LOW-FAT INGREDIENT SUBSTITUTIONS

Needed Ingredient	Substitutions
FATS AND OILS	
Butter or margarine	Reduced-calorie margarine or margarine made with canola, corn, peanut, safflower, or soybean oil; reduced-calorie stick margarine in baked products
Mayonnaise	Nonfat, reduced-fat, or low-fat mayonnaise
Oil	Safflower, soybean, corn, canola, or peanut oil in reduced amount
Salad dressing	Fat-free or oil-free dressing
Shortening	Soybean, corn, canola, or peanut oil in amount reduced by one-third
DAIRY PRODUCTS	
Cheeses: American, Cheddar, colby, Edam, or Swiss	Cheeses with 5 grams of fat or less per ounce like reduced-fat and part-skim cheeses
Cheese, cottage	Nonfat or 1% low-fat cottage cheese
Cheese, cream	Fat-free, ⅓-less-fat cheese, or tub-style light cream cheese
Cheese, ricotta	Nonfat, lite, or part-skim ricotta cheese
Cream, sour	Low-fat or nonfat sour cream; low-fat or nonfat yogurt
Cream, whipping	Chilled fat-free evaporated milk or fat-free half-and-half
Ice cream	Nonfat or low-fat frozen yogurt; nonfat or low-fat ice cream; sherbet; sorbet
Milk, whole	Fat-free, low-fat, or reduced-fat milk
MEATS, POULTRY, AND EGGS	
Bacon	Canadian bacon; turkey bacon; lean ham
Beef, ground	Extra-lean or ultra-lean ground beef; freshly ground raw turkey
Beef, lamb, pork, or veal	Chicken, turkey, or lean cuts of meat trimmed of all visible fat
Luncheon meat	Skinned, sliced turkey or chicken breast; lean ham; lean roast beef
Poultry	Skinned poultry
Tuna packed in oil	Tuna packed in water
Turkey, self-basting	Turkey basted with fat-free broth
Egg, whole	2 egg whites or ¼ cup fat-free egg substitute
MISCELLANEOUS	
Fudge sauce	Fat-free fudge sauce or chocolate syrup
Nuts	Reduce amount one-third to one-half, and toast
Soups, canned	98% fat-free or reduced-fat, reduced-sodium condensed cream soups

Salad Niçoise
(recipe, page 134)

Sea Scallops on Fettuccine
(recipe, page 28)

Cumin-Rubbed Pork Chop
(recipe, page 94)

Orange-Balsamic Chicken
(recipe, page 122)

Weight Watchers®

Quick Cooking

FOR

BUSY PEOPLE

Oxmoor House®

Library of Congress Catalog Card Number: 98-68442
ISBN: 0-8487-1855-0
Manufactured in the United States of America
First Printing 1999

Be sure to check with your health-care provider before making any changes in your diet.

Weight Watchers is a registered trademark of Weight Watchers International, Inc., and is used under license
by Healthy Living, Inc.

EDITOR-IN-CHIEF: Nancy Fitzpatrick Wyatt
SENIOR FOODS EDITOR: Katherine M. Eakin
SENIOR EDITOR, COPY AND HOMES: Olivia Kindig Wells
ART DIRECTOR: James Boone

Weight Watchers Quick Cooking for Busy People

EDITOR: Cathy A. Wesler, R.D.
CONTRIBUTING EDITOR: Deborah Garrison Lowery
ASSOCIATE ART DIRECTOR: Cynthia R. Cooper
DESIGNER: Clare T. Minges
COPY EDITOR: Keri Bradford Anderson
EDITORIAL ASSISTANT: Catherine Ritter Scholl
EDITORIAL INTERN: Jennifer Sharpton
DIRECTOR, TEST KITCHENS: Kathleen Royal Phillips
ASSISTANT DIRECTOR, TEST KITCHENS: Gayle Hays Sadler
TEST KITCHENS STAFF: Julie Christopher; Natalie E. King; L. Victoria Knowles; Regan Miller; Rebecca Mohr;
    Jan A. Smith; Kate M. Wheeler, R.D.
CONTRIBUTING RECIPE DEVELOPERS: Margaret Chason Agnew; Beth Allen; Susan Dosier; Caroline A. Grant,
    M.S., R.D.; Karen Levin; Elizabeth Tyler Luckett; Karen Mangum, M.S., R.D.; Debby Maugans Nakos;
    Lisa Hooper Talley
CONTRIBUTING INDEXER: Mary Ann Laurens
PHOTOGRAPHER: Brit Huckabay
PHOTO STYLIST: Virginia Cravens
PUBLISHING SYSTEMS ADMINISTRATOR: Rick Tucker
DIRECTOR, PRODUCTION AND DISTRIBUTION: Phillip Lee
ASSOCIATE PRODUCTION MANAGER: James E. McDaniel
PRODUCTION ASSISTANT: Faye Porter Bonner

Cover: Beef Fajitas, page 72
Back Cover: Chicken Ravioli Primavera, page 100

WE'RE HERE FOR YOU!
We at Oxmoor House are dedicated to serving
you with reliable information that expands
your imagination and enriches your life. We
welcome your comments and suggestions.
Please write us at:

Oxmoor House, Inc.
Editor, *Weight Watchers Quick Cooking
    for Busy People*
2100 Lakeshore Drive
Birmingham, AL 35209

To order additional publications, call
1-205-877-6560.

CONTENTS

INTRODUCTION

RECIPES

The Busy Person's Guide for Healthy Living

Looking for a way to squeeze in time for exercise? Trying to reduce the amount of everyday stress? We asked some busy people how they juggle exercise, family, meals, and other commitments. Here are some of their innovative, time-saving ways to keep fit and reduce stress.

Be Committed

When you exercise regularly, you'll feel better physically and mentally. Make a fitness commitment to a person, to a pet, or to a specific goal. You'll be more successful if you make yourself accountable to someone or something else.

" Get an exercise partner. My neighbor and I get up 30 minutes early and knock out two miles before the kids get up. "
—Rhonda Miller, full-time marketing coordinator and part-time student

" Several mornings a week, my husband and I set aside 20 to 30 minutes to take a brisk walk. It wakes us up and allows us time to catch up on events of the week. "
—Julie Gunter, newlywed and full-time editor who is also fixing up an old house

" My motto is, 'Discipline is remembering what you want.' I want to look good, stay at a healthy weight, reduce stress, and live the last half of my life in a healthy body. If walking 2½ miles a few times a week will provide all that, how could I not do it? "
—Vicki Baxter, bank vice-president, single mom of a teenager, and community volunteer

" After work I take care of meals and errands for my parents, who live nearby, so I exercise before work. If my errands take longer than expected in the evening, I have my exercise out of the way. "
—Donna Baldone, married copy editor and caregiver to her parents

Be Consistent

Make fitness a habit, and you'll find that it is easy to maintain. Here are some tips for turning an activity you enjoy into a regular part of your life.

" An organized class motivates me to stick to a fitness routine. I pack my gym bag the night before, change clothes at the office after work, and head straight to the gym. This routine prevents me from skipping class, because once I'm dressed, I'm going. I also plan ahead—that means preparing a slow-cooker dinner or a make-ahead-and-freeze casserole, or picking up healthy take-out food for dinner. "
—Shannon Jernigan, married book editor with sideline planning business, and community volunteer

"I get up early to run for 30 minutes and walk for 45 minutes. Exercising early helps me make sure it happens. After keeping this routine for a few months, it's become a habit and I no longer think much about whether to do it or not. Then three days a week I take a step aerobics class during my lunch hour—it keeps me energized for the afternoon and prevents me from eating a big lunch."

—Lauren Brooks, full-time editorial assistant, church member, and quilt guild member

"I do abdominal crunches and stretches every morning before I get dressed. With a new baby it would be easy to let exercise take a backseat, so this morning routine helps me get exercise into my day. If my schedule permits, I walk a mile or two during my lunch hour. That way, I can spend the rest of my after-work free time with my daughter."

—Ann Marie Harvey, working mom of a newborn baby

BE CREATIVE

Look for unique and fun ways to fulfill your day-to-day commitments. Plan ahead and you'll be able to find time for exercise and healthy eating without being stressed or feeling guilty. Here are some tips to help.

"I like to exercise with a friend after work at a nearby park, so I plan meals and buy groceries for the week on Sundays; then I don't miss my planned exercise time because of having to rush to the grocery store after work."

—Adrienne Davis, editor, newlywed, and community volunteer

"I try to do most of my cooking during the weekend or on one weeknight. This way, putting meals together during the work week is quicker and easier and I have more time in the evening."

—Stacey Geary, single professional, active member of a book club and supper club

"I walk every morning with my best friend while the kids are still asleep and my husband is getting ready for work. To avoid a morning rush, I set out breakfast dishes and cereal boxes the night before. I fill bottles and sipper cups ahead and keep them in the refrigerator. Then breakfast is a snap to serve, whether it's me or my husband doing the serving."

—Whitney Pickering, working mother of two toddlers and minister's wife

"I work an early flextime schedule so I can get home, have a little time to unwind, and have dinner ready by the time my husband gets home. That way, we have plenty of time left for exercising. I also change into my workout clothes as soon as I get home—before cooking, opening mail, or turning on the television. I'm much more likely to work out if I'm already dressed to exercise."

—Emily Parrish, full-time graphic designer and part-time entrepreneur

About These Recipes

Weight Watchers° Quick Cooking for Busy People gives you the
nutrition facts you want to know. To make your life easier, we've provided
the following useful information with every recipe:

- A number calculated through **POINTS**° Food System, an integral part of Weight Watchers *1•2•3 Success*° Weight Loss Plan
- Diabetic exchange values for those who use them as a guide for planning meals
- A complete nutrient analysis per serving

POINTS Food System

Every recipe in the book includes a
number assigned through **POINTS** value.
This system uses a formula based on the
calorie, fat, and fiber content of the food.
Foods with more calories and fat (like
a slice of pepperoni pizza) receive high
numbers, while fruits and vegetables receive
low numbers. For more information about
the *1•2•3 Success* Weight Loss Plan and
the Weight Watchers meeting nearest you,
call 1-800-651-6000.

Diabetic Exchanges

Exchange values are provided for people
who use them for calorie-controlled diets
and for people with diabetes. All foods with-
in a certain group contain approximately the
same amount of nutrients and calories, so
one serving of a food from a food group can
be substituted or exchanged for one serving
of any other item on the list.

The food groups are meat, starch, veg-
etable, fruit, fat, and milk. The exchange
values are based on the *Exchange Lists for*
Meal Planning developed by the American
Diabetes Association and the American
Dietetic Association.

Nutritional Analyses

Each recipe has a complete list of nutrients; numbers are based on these assumptions.

- Unless otherwise indicated, meat, poultry, and fish refer to skinned, boned,
  and cooked servings.
- When we give a range for an ingredient
  (3 to 3½ cups flour, for instance), we
  calculate using the lesser amount.
- Some alcohol calories evaporate during
  heating; the analysis reflects that.
- Only the amount of marinade absorbed
  by the food is used in calculation.
- Garnishes and optional ingredients are
  not included in analysis.

The nutritional values used in our calcu-
lations either come from a computer pro-
gram by Computrition, Inc., or are provided
by food manufacturers.

fish & shellfish

Flounder in Foil Pouches

POINTS
<u></u>
3

EXCHANGES
3 Very Lean Meat
1 Vegetable

PER SERVING
Calories 138
Carbohydrate 5.6g
Fat 2.7g (saturated 0.5g)
Fiber 1.7g
Protein 22.2g
Cholesterol 54mg
Sodium 254mg
Calcium 47mg
Iron 1.0mg

4   green onions, cut into 1-inch pieces
2   medium carrots, scraped and cut into thin strips
1   tablespoon fresh lemon juice
1   teaspoon olive oil
¼   teaspoon paprika
Cooking spray
4   (4-ounce) flounder fillets
¼   teaspoon salt
4   thin slices lemon

1. Place green onions and carrot strips in a 2-cup glass measuring cup; cover with heavy-duty plastic wrap, and microwave at HIGH 3 minutes. Drain and set aside.

2. Meanwhile, combine lemon juice, olive oil, and paprika in a small bowl; stir well.

3. Cut four 15-inch squares of aluminum foil. Place foil on a large baking sheet. Lightly coat squares with cooking spray. Place a fillet in center of each square; top fillets evenly with green onion mixture. Spoon lemon juice mixture evenly over fillets and green onion mixture; sprinkle with salt. Top each serving with a lemon slice. Fold foil over fillets and vegetables, and crimp edges to seal.

4. Bake at 400° for 8 minutes. Transfer pouches to individual serving plates; cut an X in top of each pouch, and fold cut edges back. Yield: 4 servings.

 FOR A QUICK MEAL: Serve with parslied rice and Peachy Parfaits (page 187).

Flounder with Peppers and Green Onions

2	teaspoons reduced-calorie margarine
⅓	cup sliced green onions
1	teaspoon bottled minced garlic
1	small sweet red pepper, cut into thin strips
1	pound flounder fillets, cut into 4 pieces
3	tablespoons dry white wine
½	teaspoon grated lime rind
2	tablespoons fresh lime juice

POINTS

3

EXCHANGES

3 Very Lean Meat

1 Vegetable

PER SERVING

Calories 134

Carbohydrate 3.3g

Fat 2.7g (saturated 0.3g)

Fiber 0.7g

Protein 21.9g

Cholesterol 54mg

Sodium 113mg

Calcium 30mg

Iron 1.0mg

1. Melt margarine in a large nonstick skillet over medium-high heat. Add green onions, garlic, and pepper strips; cook 2 minutes, stirring often.

2. Add fish, and cook 2 minutes on each side. Sprinkle wine, lime rind, and lime juice over fish. Cover, reduce heat, and simmer 3 minutes or until fish flakes easily when tested with a fork. Carefully remove fish to a serving platter; top with pepper mixture. Yield: 4 servings.

 FOR A QUICK MEAL: Serve with Greek Vegetable Salad (page 183) and warm French bread.

Spicy Grouper Fillets *(photo, page 23)*

POINTS

3

EXCHANGES

3 Very Lean Meat

PER SERVING

Calories 132

Carbohydrate 3.5g

Fat 2.5g (saturated 0.4g)

Fiber 0.2g

Protein 22.5g

Cholesterol 42mg

Sodium 354mg

Calcium 35mg

Iron 1.3mg

2 tablespoons all-purpose flour
½ teaspoon paprika
½ teaspoon salt
¼ teaspoon ground red pepper
4 (4-ounce) grouper fillets
Cooking spray
1 teaspoon olive oil
1 teaspoon minced garlic
Lemon wedges (optional)

1. Combine first 4 ingredients in a large heavy-duty, zip-top plastic bag. Add fish, and turn gently to coat.

2. Coat a large nonstick skillet with cooking spray; add oil, and place skillet over medium heat until hot. Add garlic; cook, stirring constantly, 30 seconds. Add fish; cook 3 minutes on each side or until fish flakes easily when tested with a fork, removing pieces as they are done. Serve with lemon wedges, if desired. Yield: 4 servings.

 FOR A QUICK MEAL: Serve with Asian Coleslaw (page 183) and strawberry sorbet.

Grilled Grouper with Pineapple Salsa

1   (15-ounce) can pineapple tidbits in juice, drained
1   small sweet red pepper, finely chopped (about ½ cup)
2   tablespoons chopped fresh mint or parsley
1   tablespoon lime juice
2   teaspoons finely chopped fresh jalapeño pepper
1   teaspoon peeled, grated gingerroot or ¼ teaspoon ground
      ginger
½   teaspoon salt, divided
¼   teaspoon ground black pepper
4   (4-ounce) grouper fillets
Cooking spray

POINTS

3

EXCHANGES

3 Very Lean Meat

1 Fruit

PER SERVING

Calories 155

Carbohydrate 12.1g

Fat 1.4g (saturated 0.3g)

Fiber 1.4g

Protein 22.2g

Cholesterol 42mg

Sodium 341mg

Calcium 29mg

Iron 1.5mg

1. Combine first 6 ingredients in a small bowl; stir in ¼ teaspoon salt. Cover and set aside; chill overnight, if desired.

2. Sprinkle remaining ¼ teaspoon salt and ¼ teaspoon ground black pepper over fish; coat lightly with cooking spray.

3. Coat grill rack with cooking spray; place on grill over medium-hot coals (350° to 400°). Arrange fish on rack or in a grill basket coated with cooking spray; grill, uncovered, 5 minutes on each side or until fish flakes easily when tested with a fork. Remove fish from grill, and top with pineapple mixture. Yield: 4 servings.

 FOR A QUICK MEAL: Serve with steamed Sugar Snap peas and warm whole wheat rolls.

Newport Orange Roughy

POINTS

2

EXCHANGES

3 Very Lean Meat

PER SERVING

Calories 107

Carbohydrate 2.6g

Fat 3.4g (saturated 0.1g)

Fiber 0.3g

Protein 17.3g

Cholesterol 23mg

Sodium 91mg

Calcium 23mg

Iron 0.4mg

6   (4-ounce) orange roughy fillets

Cooking spray

2   tablespoons lemon juice

1   tablespoon reduced-calorie margarine, melted

2   teaspoons salt-free garlic and herb seasoning (such as
     Mrs. Dash)

1   (2-ounce) jar diced pimiento, drained

2   tablespoons sliced almonds

1. Arrange fish in a single layer on rack of a broiler pan coated with cooking spray. Combine lemon juice and next 3 ingredients in a small bowl. Drizzle evenly over fish.

2. Broil fish 5½ inches from heat 12 minutes or until fish flakes easily when tested with a fork. Sprinkle fish with almonds the last minute of broiling. Yield: 6 servings.

 FOR A QUICK MEAL: Serve with Italian Antipasto Salad (page 183) and Italian bread.

Spicy Lemon Red Snapper

4   (4-ounce) red snapper fillets
¼   cup fresh lemon juice
1   teaspoon black and red pepper blend (such as McCormick's)
1   teaspoon dry mustard
1   teaspoon onion powder
1   teaspoon dried thyme
Cooking spray
Lemon wedges (optional)

POINTS

3

EXCHANGES

3 Very Lean Meat

PER SERVING

Calories 121
Carbohydrate 1.1g
Fat 1.9g (saturated 0.3g)
Fiber 0.1g
Protein 23.5g
Cholesterol 42mg
Sodium 51mg
Calcium 45mg
Iron 0.7mg

1. Place fish in a large shallow dish; pour lemon juice over fish. Let stand 5 minutes.

2. While fish marinates, combine pepper blend and next 3 ingredients. Remove fish from lemon juice, discarding juice. Rub pepper mixture over both sides of fillets.

3. Coat grill rack with cooking spray; place on grill over medium-hot coals (350° to 400°). Place fish on rack or in a grill basket coated with cooking spray; grill, covered, 3 minutes on each side or until fish flakes easily when tested with a fork. Serve with lemon wedges, if desired. Yield: 4 servings.

 FOR A QUICK MEAL: Serve with green beans and corn muffins.

Wine-Poached Salmon

POINTS

5

EXCHANGES

3 Lean Meat

PER SERVING

Calories 204

Carbohydrate 1.4g

Fat 9.7g (saturated 1.7g)

Fiber 0.1g

Protein 25.3g

Cholesterol 77mg

Sodium 69mg

Calcium 12mg

Iron 0.6mg

1   cup canned no-salt-added chicken broth

¼   cup dry white wine

1   cup slivered onion (about 1 small)

2   teaspoons dried dillweed or 2 tablespoons chopped fresh dillweed

4   (4-ounce) skinless salmon fillets

½   cup nonfat sour cream

¼   cup chopped cucumber (about ½ small)

1   teaspoon dried dillweed or 1 tablespoon chopped fresh dillweed

1. Bring first 4 ingredients to a boil in a large nonstick skillet. Reduce heat to medium-low, and add fish; cover and simmer 7 minutes or until fish is firm when touched in center. Remove from heat; cover and let stand 3 minutes.

2. While fish cooks, combine sour cream, cucumber, and 1 teaspoon dillweed in a small bowl. Remove salmon and onion from poaching liquid, using a slotted spoon; top with sour cream mixture. Yield: 4 servings.

 FOR A QUICK MEAL: Serve with steamed asparagus. For dessert, prepare Strawberry Trifle (page 187) while the salmon cooks.

Tortellini and Salmon Dinner

Cooking spray
1   (8-ounce) package sliced fresh mushrooms
1½   cups fat-free refrigerated marinara sauce
½   teaspoon olive oil
3   cloves garlic, thinly sliced
4   (4-ounce) skinless salmon fillets
1   (9-ounce) package refrigerated spinach- and cheese-filled
     tortellini, uncooked

POINTS
9

EXCHANGES
3 Lean Meat
2½ Starch
1 Vegetable

PER SERVING
Calories 416
Carbohydrate 43.5g
Fat 11.5g (saturated 3.6g)
Fiber 3.8g
Protein 34.9g
Cholesterol 67mg
Sodium 400mg
Calcium 69mg
Iron 1.9mg

1. Coat a large saucepan with cooking spray; place over medium-high heat until hot. Add mushrooms, and cook, stirring often, 5 minutes or until tender. Stir in marinara sauce, and set aside.

2. Pour oil into a large nonstick skillet; place over medium-high heat. Add garlic, and cook, stirring constantly, 30 seconds. Add fish, and cook, turning once, 9 minutes or until fish flakes easily when tested with a fork.

3. While fish cooks, cook pasta according to package directions, omitting salt. Drain pasta, and stir into mushroom mixture. Place over medium-high heat; cook 1 minute or until thoroughly heated, stirring often. Spoon pasta mixture evenly onto individual serving plates; arrange fish over pasta. Yield: 4 servings.

FOR A QUICK MEAL: This is a one-dish meal in itself, but a simple tossed green salad would make a good complementary side dish.

Teriyaki-Glazed Salmon with Peach Salsa *(photo, facing page)*

POINTS

5

EXCHANGES

3 Lean Meat

1 Fruit

PER SERVING

Calories 233

Carbohydrate 10.4g

Fat 10.2g (saturated 1.7g)

Fiber 0.8g

Protein 24.5g

Cholesterol 77mg

Sodium 140mg

Calcium 11mg

Iron 0.6mg

3   tablespoons low-sodium teriyaki sauce
2   tablespoons lime juice
1½ tablespoons honey
4   (4-ounce) skinless salmon fillets
1½ cups frozen peach slices, thawed and chopped, or 1½ cups
       drained and chopped canned peaches
¼   cup minced fresh cilantro or mint
2   teaspoons honey
1   teaspoon lime juice
Cooking spray

1. Combine first 3 ingredients in a shallow dish; stir well. Add fish, and let stand 5 minutes.

2. While fish marinates, combine peach slices and next 3 ingredients in a small bowl; stir well. Set aside.

3. Coat grill rack with cooking spray; place on grill over medium-hot coals (350° to 400°). Remove fish from marinade, discarding marinade. Place fish on rack or in a grill basket coated with cooking spray; grill, uncovered, 3 to 5 minutes on each side or until fish flakes easily when tested with a fork. Remove fish from grill, and top with peach mixture. Yield: 4 servings.

 FOR A QUICK MEAL: Serve with steamed asparagus. For extra flavor, drizzle lemon juice over the asparagus.

Jamaican Shrimp and
Pineapple Kabob
(recipe, page 32)

Spicy Grouper Fillet
(recipe, page 14)

Dilled Shrimp with
Angel Hair Pasta
(recipe, page 31)

Greek Snapper

Cooking spray
½   cup chopped onion (about ¾ small)
½   cup chopped green pepper (about ½ medium)
1   teaspoon minced garlic
1   (14½-ounce) can no-salt-added stewed tomatoes, undrained
1   tablespoon fresh lemon juice
1   teaspoon Greek seasoning
½   teaspoon dried oregano
4   (4-ounce) red snapper fillets
1   ounce crumbled feta cheese

POINTS

4

EXCHANGES

3 Very Lean Meat
2 Vegetable

PER SERVING

Calories 176
Carbohydrate 10.1g
Fat 3.3g (saturated 1.4g)
Fiber 1.1g
Protein 25.8g
Cholesterol 48mg
Sodium 412mg
Calcium 110mg
Iron 1.2mg

1. Coat a large nonstick skillet with cooking spray; place over medium-high heat until hot. Add onion, green pepper, and garlic; cook, stirring constantly, until tender. Add tomatoes and next 3 ingredients; bring to a boil.

2. Reduce heat, and add fish, spooning tomato mixture over fish. Cover and simmer 15 minutes or until fish flakes easily when tested with a fork. Transfer fish to individual serving plates; spoon tomato mixture evenly over fish, and sprinkle with feta cheese. Yield: 4 servings.

 FOR A QUICK MEAL: Serve with basmati rice and focaccia wedges.

Grilled Tuna Skewers

POINTS

5

EXCHANGES

3 Lean Meat

1 Vegetable

1 Fruit

PER SERVING

Calories 254

Carbohydrate 18.5g

Fat 7.3g (saturated 1.6g)

Fiber 2.4g

Protein 27.1g

Cholesterol 43mg

Sodium 340mg

Calcium 30mg

Iron 2.4mg

8	ounces tuna steaks, trimmed and cut into 1-inch pieces
1	medium-size green pepper, cut into 1-inch pieces (about 1 cup)
1	cup pineapple chunks
¼	cup lemon juice
¼	cup dry white wine
2	teaspoons minced garlic
1	teaspoon dried oregano
1	teaspoon olive oil
½	teaspoon salt

Cooking spray

1. Thread first 3 ingredients alternately onto four 12-inch metal skewers. Combine lemon juice and next 5 ingredients, stirring well; brush over kabobs.

2. Coat grill rack with cooking spray; place on grill over medium-hot coals (350° to 400°). Place kabobs on rack; grill, covered, 8 to 12 minutes or until tuna flakes easily when tested with a fork, turning and basting with lemon juice mixture. Yield: 2 servings.

 FOR A QUICK MEAL: Serve with couscous and Sweet-and-Spicy Bean Toss (page 183).

Creamy Skillet Tuna Casserole

1   (10¾-ounce) can reduced-fat, reduced-sodium cream of mushroom soup
½   cup canned fat-free, reduced-sodium chicken broth
½   cup evaporated fat-free milk
¼   teaspoon pepper
¾   cup frozen diced onion
3   cups cooked egg noodles (cooked without salt or fat)
1   cup frozen English peas
2   (6-ounce) cans low-sodium tuna in water, drained
1   (2-ounce) jar diced pimiento, drained
¼   cup grated Parmesan cheese

POINTS

5

EXCHANGES

2 Lean Meat

2½ Starch

PER SERVING

Calories 292

Carbohydrate 38.8g

Fat 4.4g (saturated 2.1g)

Fiber 3.9g

Protein 22.7g

Cholesterol 54mg

Sodium 459mg

Calcium 194mg

Iron 2.9mg

1. Combine first 4 ingredients in a large skillet, stirring until smooth. Stir in onion; bring to a boil over medium heat, stirring often. Reduce heat, and simmer, uncovered, 5 minutes or until onion is tender.

2. Stir in noodles and next 3 ingredients. Simmer, uncovered, 5 minutes or until thoroughly heated, stirring occasionally. Spoon onto individual serving plates, and sprinkle evenly with cheese. Yield: 5 servings.

 FOR A QUICK MEAL: Serve with a mixed green salad and Apple Pie Sundae (page 186).

Sea Scallops on Fettuccine *(photo, page 2)*

POINTS

6

EXCHANGES

3 Very Lean Meat

2 Starch

½ Fruit

PER SERVING

Calories 295

Carbohydrate 39.1g

Fat 2.4g (saturated 0.1g)

Fiber 2.2g

Protein 26.7g

Cholesterol 38mg

Sodium 326mg

Calcium 70mg

Iron 2.2mg

2　teaspoons grated lime rind, divided
½　cup fresh lime juice
½　cup fresh orange juice
½　teaspoon ground white pepper
1　pound sea scallops, halved lengthwise
1　(9-ounce) package refrigerated spinach fettuccine
Cooking spray
¾　cup sliced green onions (about 3 large)

1. Combine 1 teaspoon lime rind and next 3 ingredients in a shallow dish; add scallops, and let stand 5 minutes, turning once.

2. While scallops marinate, cook pasta according to package directions, omitting salt and fat. Drain well. Set aside; keep warm.

3. Remove scallops from marinade, reserving marinade. Coat a large nonstick skillet with cooking spray; place over medium-high heat until hot. Add scallops; cook 1 minute on each side or until lightly browned. Remove scallops from skillet; set aside, and keep warm. Add marinade mixture to skillet, and cook 1 minute, stirring to scrape particles that cling to bottom of skillet.

4. Combine pasta and green onions in a large bowl. Add scallops and marinade mixture to pasta mixture; toss lightly. Sprinkle with remaining 1 teaspoon lime rind. Yield: 4 servings.

 FOR A QUICK MEAL: Serve with Minted Strawberry-Pineapple Salad (page 182) and Italian bread.

Thai Shrimp with Basil

1   pound peeled, deveined medium-size fresh shrimp

2   teaspoons peeled, minced gingerroot

Garlic-flavored cooking spray

1   cup (1½-inch-long) carrot sticks (half of an 8-ounce package
     carrot sticks)

¼   teaspoon dried crushed red pepper

6   ounces fresh snow pea pods, trimmed

⅓   cup light teriyaki sauce

¼   cup thinly sliced fresh basil

1. Toss shrimp with gingerroot; set aside.

2. Coat a large nonstick skillet with cooking spray; place over medium-high heat until hot. Add carrot sticks, and cook 2 minutes, stirring often. Add shrimp mixture; stir-fry 2 minutes. Add red pepper, snow peas, and teriyaki sauce; stir-fry 2 minutes or until shrimp turn pink. Stir in basil. Yield: 4 (1-cup) servings.

FOR A QUICK MEAL: Serve with brown rice and soft garlic breadsticks.

POINTS

3

EXCHANGES

3 Very Lean Meat

2 Vegetable

PER SERVING

Calories 174

Carbohydrate 11.4g

Fat 2.3g (saturated 0.4g)

Fiber 2.1g

Protein 25.0g

Cholesterol 172mg

Sodium 604mg

Calcium 88mg

Iron 3.8mg

Skillet Barbecued Shrimp

POINTS
6

EXCHANGES
3 Very Lean Meat
2½ Starch

PER SERVING
Calories 293
Carbohydrate 39.6g
Fat 2.4g (saturated 0.4g)
Fiber 0.8g
Protein 26.4g
Cholesterol 172mg
Sodium 629mg
Calcium 79mg
Iron 4.1mg

1   family-size bag quick-cooking boil-in-bag rice or 3 cups hot cooked rice

1   pound peeled, deveined large fresh shrimp

2   teaspoons no-salt-added Creole seasoning (such as Tony Chachere's)

Cooking spray

½   cup chili sauce (such as Heinz)

½   teaspoon hot sauce

1. Cook rice according to package directions, omitting salt and fat.

2. While rice cooks, toss shrimp with Creole seasoning. Coat a large nonstick skillet with cooking spray; place over medium-high heat until hot. Add shrimp; cook 3 to 5 minutes or until shrimp turn pink, stirring often. Add chili sauce and hot sauce; reduce heat, and cook 2 minutes. Serve over rice. Yield: 4 servings.

FOR A QUICK MEAL: Serve with Lemon-Pepper Corn on the Cob (page 184) and a spinach-orange salad. For fresh citrus flavor, toss orange sections with the spinach before drizzling with fat-free poppy seed dressing.

Dilled Shrimp with Angel Hair Pasta *(photo, page 24)*

6   ounces angel hair pasta, uncooked

2   tablespoons reduced-calorie margarine

¾   cup sliced green onions (about 3 large)

3   tablespoons fresh lemon juice (1 large)

2   large cloves garlic, minced

1   pound peeled, deveined large fresh shrimp

½   cup fat-free half-and-half or fat-free evaporated milk

¼   cup tub-style light cream cheese

2   tablespoons chopped fresh dillweed or 1½ teaspoons dried
     dillweed

POINTS

8

EXCHANGES

3 Very Lean Meat

2½ Starch

½ Fat

PER SERVING

Calories 368

Carbohydrate 37.4g

Fat 9.5g (saturated 1.8g)

Fiber 0.3g

Protein 31.0g

Cholesterol 180mg

Sodium 366mg

Calcium 115mg

Iron 3.7mg

1. Cook pasta according to package directions, omitting salt and fat. Drain.

2. While pasta cooks, melt margarine in a large nonstick skillet over medium-high heat. Add green onions, lemon juice, and garlic; cook 2 minutes, stirring often. Add shrimp, and cook 5 minutes or until shrimp turn pink. Remove shrimp from skillet; set aside.

3. Add half-and-half, cream cheese, and dillweed to skillet, stirring until smooth. Cook 1 to 2 minutes or until mixture is bubbly. Return shrimp to skillet, and cook until thoroughly heated. Combine shrimp mixture and pasta, tossing well. Serve immediately. Yield: 4 servings.

FOR A QUICK MEAL: Serve with Fruited Spinach Salad (page 182) and warm sourdough bread.

Jamaican Shrimp and Pineapple Kabobs *(photo, page 22)*

POINTS

3

EXCHANGES

2 Very Lean Meat

1 Vegetable

1 Fruit

PER SERVING

Calories 168

Carbohydrate 25.4g

Fat 1.2g (saturated 0.2g)

Fiber 1.2g

Protein 14.5g

Cholesterol 131mg

Sodium 461mg

Calcium 31mg

Iron 2.7mg

⅓ cup steak sauce

¼ cup guava jelly, pineapple preserves, or plum jelly

1 teaspoon hot sauce (optional)

¾ pound peeled, deveined large shrimp

1 cup packaged fresh cubed pineapple

1 green or sweet red pepper, cut into 1-inch pieces (about 1½ cups)

Cooking spray

1. Combine steak sauce, guava jelly, and, if desired, hot sauce; stir well. Thread shrimp, pineapple, and pepper alternately onto four 10-inch skewers; brush with half of sauce mixture.

2. Coat a grill rack with cooking spray; place on grill over medium-hot coals (350° to 400°). Place kabobs on rack; grill, covered, 6 minutes or until shrimp turn pink and pepper is crisp-tender, turning once. Brush with remaining sauce mixture, and serve immediately. Yield: 4 servings.

> FOR A QUICK MEAL: For a side dish, toss hot cooked orzo with no-salt-added chicken broth. For a vegetable, cut zucchini lengthwise into quarters and grill until crisp-tender.

meatless main dishes

RECIPE TIME: 16 minutes

Mediterranean Pizza

POINTS
6

EXCHANGES
½ Medium-Fat Meat
2 Starch
1 Vegetable
1 Fat

PER SERVING
Calories 265
Carbohydrate 34.0g
Fat 9.7g (saturated 2.8g)
Fiber 2.7g
Protein 11.9g
Cholesterol 2mg
Sodium 561mg
Calcium 220mg
Iron 1.9mg

1 (7-ounce) container refrigerated hummus
1 (10-ounce) thin crust Italian bread shell (such as Boboli)
1 (7-ounce) jar roasted red peppers, drained and chopped
1 (14½-ounce) can quartered artichoke hearts, drained and
     coarsely chopped
4 kalamata olives, pitted and chopped
2 ounces crumbled tomato- and basil-flavored feta cheese

1. Spread hummus over bread shell; arrange peppers and remaining ingredients over hummus.

2. Bake at 450° for 12 to 14 minutes or until cheese softens and pizza is thoroughly heated. Yield: 6 servings.

 FOR A QUICK MEAL: Serve with a romaine lettuce salad tossed with fat-free raspberry vinaigrette.

RECIPE TIME: 18 minutes

Tomato-Basil Pizza *(photo, page 41)*

1   (10-ounce) thin crust Italian bread shell (such as Boboli)
⅓   cup pizza sauce
2   medium-size ripe tomatoes, thinly sliced
2   teaspoons dried basil or 2 tablespoons chopped fresh basil
¼   cup grated Parmesan cheese
1   cup (4 ounces) shredded reduced-fat Italian cheese blend or
    mozzarella cheese

1. Place bread shell on a baking sheet; spread with pizza sauce. Top bread shell with tomato slices; sprinkle with basil and Parmesan cheese.

2. Bake at 450° for 10 minutes. Sprinkle with shredded cheese; bake 2 to 3 additional minutes or until crust is golden and cheese melts. Cut into 8 wedges. Yield: 4 servings.

 FOR A QUICK MEAL: Serve with a fresh fruit salad or watermelon wedges.

POINTS
7

EXCHANGES
2 Lean Meat
2 Starch
1 Vegetable
1 Fat

PER SERVING
Calories 326
Carbohydrate 36.4g
Fat 10.9g (saturated 4.6g)
Fiber 2.5g
Protein 22.0g
Cholesterol 22mg
Sodium 821mg
Calcium 422mg
Iron 1.7mg

Egg Olé Burritos

POINTS

4

EXCHANGES

1 Lean Meat

1½ Starch

PER SERVING

Calories 200

Carbohydrate 20.1g

Fat 3.6g (saturated 0.8g)

Fiber 1.6g

Protein 11.2g

Cholesterol 5mg

Sodium 685mg

Calcium 86mg

Iron 1.5mg

1 (8-ounce) carton fat-free egg substitute
¼ teaspoon salt
¼ teaspoon pepper
Cooking spray
¼ cup (1 ounce) shredded reduced-fat Cheddar cheese
4 (8-inch) flour tortillas
½ cup thick and chunky salsa
¼ cup nonfat sour cream
2 tablespoons chopped fresh cilantro or parsley

1. Combine first 3 ingredients in a small bowl. Coat a large non-stick skillet with cooking spray; place over medium heat until hot. Add egg mixture; cook until mixture is softly set, stirring often. Remove from heat, and top with cheese.

2. Spoon egg substitute mixture evenly over tortillas; top with salsa, sour cream, and cilantro. Roll up tortillas; place, seam side down, on a serving platter. Yield: 4 servings.

 FOR A QUICK MEAL: Serve with steamed green beans and cantaloupe slices.

RECIPE TIME: 10 minutes

Cheese and Vegetable Omelet

Butter-flavored cooking spray
1¾ cups finely chopped zucchini (about 1 small)
¼ teaspoon dried dillweed
1 (8-ounce) carton fat-free egg substitute
⅓ cup thinly sliced green onions
¼ teaspoon freshly ground pepper
⅛ teaspoon salt
½ cup (2 ounces) reduced-fat shredded Cheddar cheese

POINTS

4

EXCHANGES

3 Lean Meat

1 Vegetable

PER SERVING

Calories 168
Carbohydrate 6.9g
Fat 5.9g (saturated 3.2g)
Fiber 1.0g
Protein 21.9g
Cholesterol 18mg
Sodium 542mg
Calcium 293mg
Iron 3.0mg

1. Coat a 10-inch nonstick skillet with cooking spray; place over medium-high heat until hot. Add zucchini, and cook 4 minutes or until crisp-tender, stirring occasionally. Stir in dillweed; remove mixture from skillet, and set aside. Wipe skillet with paper towels.

2. Coat skillet with cooking spray; place over medium-high heat until hot. Combine egg substitute and next 3 ingredients, stirring well. Add egg substitute mixture to skillet, and cook 2 minutes. Carefully lift edges of omelet using a spatula; allow uncooked portion to flow underneath cooked portion. Cook 2 additional minutes or until center is almost set.

3. Spoon cheese and zucchini mixture down center of omelet. Fold omelet in half. Reduce heat to low; cook 1 additional minute or until cheese melts and omelet is set. Yield: 2 servings.

 FOR A QUICK MEAL: Serve with toasted English muffins and sliced tomatoes.

Tomato-Feta Omelet *(photo, page 61)*

POINTS

2

EXCHANGES

2 Lean Meat

1 Vegetable

PER SERVING

Calories 117

Carbohydrate 6.5g

Fat 3.4g (saturated 2.2g)

Fiber 1.0g

Protein 14.7g

Cholesterol 13mg

Sodium 490mg

Calcium 116mg

Iron 2.6mg

1   (8-ounce) carton fat-free egg substitute
⅛   teaspoon salt
⅛   teaspoon pepper
Olive oil-flavored cooking spray
2   tablespoons finely chopped purple onion
2   medium plum tomatoes, chopped
¼   cup crumbled garlic- and herb-flavored feta cheese

1. Combine first 3 ingredients in a medium bowl, stirring well with a wire whisk.

2. Coat a medium nonstick skillet with cooking spray; place over medium-high heat until hot. Add onion, and sauté until tender; remove from skillet, and set aside. Reduce heat to medium; add egg substitute mixture to skillet. Carefully lift edges of omelet using a spatula; allow uncooked portion to flow underneath cooked portion. Cook until omelet is softly set; remove from heat.

3. Spoon onion, tomato, and cheese onto center of omelet. Fold one-third of omelet over filling, and slide omelet onto a plate; fold remaining one-third omelet over top. Yield: 2 servings.

 FOR A QUICK MEAL: Serve with Fruited Spinach Salad (page 182) and warm pita bread.

Cheese and Chile Tortilla Stack

3   (8-inch) fat-free flour tortillas
Cooking spray
1½ cups (6 ounces) shredded part-skim mozzarella cheese
1   tablespoon plus 1 teaspoon chopped canned jalapeño peppers, drained
¾   cup chopped green onions (about 3), divided
2   cups shredded iceberg lettuce
¼   cup nonfat sour cream
¼   cup thick and chunky salsa
2   tablespoons chopped fresh cilantro or parsley

POINTS
6

EXCHANGES
2 Medium-Fat Meat
1 Starch
2 Vegetable

PER SERVING
Calories 298
Carbohydrate 32.2g
Fat 9.2g (saturated 5.8g)
Fiber 4.4g
Protein 20.4g
Cholesterol 33mg
Sodium 603mg
Calcium 397mg
Iron 1.2mg

1. Place 1 tortilla on a baking sheet coated with cooking spray; sprinkle with ¾ cup cheese, 2 teaspoons jalapeño pepper, and ¼ cup green onions. Top with another tortilla, pressing down gently. Sprinkle with remaining cheese, remaining pepper, and ¼ cup green onions. Top with remaining tortilla, pressing down gently. Coat tortilla stack with cooking spray.

2. Bake at 400° for 6 to 8 minutes or until cheese melts; remove from oven, and transfer to a serving platter. Top with lettuce, sour cream, and salsa. Sprinkle with remaining ¼ cup green onions and cilantro. Yield: 3 servings.

FOR A QUICK MEAL: Serve with a fruit plate of sliced pears and red grapes. Sprinkle the pear slices with lime juice, and top with grapes. Dust with a little powdered sugar right before serving.

Brown Rice-Vegetable Burritos

POINTS
5

EXCHANGES
1 Very Lean Meat
3 Starch
1 Vegetable

PER SERVING
Calories 308
Carbohydrate 59.7g
Fat 1.6g (saturated 0.0g)
Fiber 8.0g
Protein 13.2g
Cholesterol 0mg
Sodium 510mg
Calcium 66mg
Iron 1.5mg

1   (3-ounce) bag quick-cooking brown rice, uncooked (such as Success)
Cooking spray
1   cup diced yellow squash
¼   cup chopped purple onion
1   cup drained canned chick-peas (garbanzo beans)
½   cup diced tomato
6   (8-inch) fat-free flour tortillas
1   (12-ounce) jar fat-free black bean dip

1. Cook rice according to package directions; set aside to drain.

2. While rice cooks, coat a large nonstick skillet with cooking spray; place over medium-high heat until hot. Add squash and onion; cook 5 minutes or until crisp-tender, stirring often. Combine squash mixture, chick-peas, tomato, and cooked rice, stirring gently.

3. Wrap tortillas in heavy-duty plastic wrap, and microwave at HIGH 1 minute or until warm. Spread 2 tablespoons bean dip over each tortilla. Spoon ¾ cup rice mixture down center of each tortilla; fold in 1 side, and roll up. Yield: 6 servings.

FOR A QUICK MEAL: Serve with pineapple wedges and steamed corn on the cob. For a flavor kick, sprinkle salt-free lemon-pepper seasoning on the corn.

Tomato-Basil Pizza
(recipe, page 35)

Fiesta Black Beans over Rice
(recipe, page 48)

Linguine with Vegetables
and Asiago Cheese
(recipe, page 53)

Veggie-Bean Tostadas *(photo, facing page)*

Cooking spray

1½ cups packaged fresh sliced mushrooms

1½ cups packaged fresh broccoli flowerets

1   cup packaged fresh shredded carrots

½   cup picante sauce

2   tablespoons water

1   (16-ounce) can fat-free refried beans

4   (6-inch) corn tortillas

1   cup (4 ounces) shredded reduced-fat four-cheese Mexican
     cheese blend (such as Sargento)

1½ tablespoons nonfat sour cream (optional)

¼   cup chopped fresh cilantro (optional)

½   cup picante sauce (optional)

POINTS

4

EXCHANGES

2 Lean Meat

1 Starch

2 Vegetable

PER SERVING

Calories 226

Carbohydrate 30.1g

Fat 7.1g (saturated 4.0g)

Fiber 8.0g

Protein 16.0g

Cholesterol 10mg

Sodium 1015mg

Calcium 287mg

Iron 2.2mg

1. Coat a large nonstick skillet with cooking spray; place skillet over medium-high heat until hot. Add mushrooms and next 4 ingredients; cover and simmer 7 minutes or until vegetables are crisp-tender.

2. While vegetable mixture cooks, heat beans according to directions on label. Place tortillas on baking sheet; broil 5½ inches from heat 1 minute on each side or until crisp and golden. Place tortillas on individual serving plates. Top with beans, vegetables, cheese, and, if desired, sour cream, cilantro, and picante sauce. Yield: 4 servings.

 FOR A QUICK MEAL: Serve with Cinnamon-Spiced Bananas (page 186).

Tortilla and Black Bean Casserole

POINTS

4

EXCHANGES

1 Medium-Fat Meat

1½ Starch

1 Vegetable

PER SERVING

Calories 226

Carbohydrate 29.7g

Fat 6.8g (saturated 3.8g)

Fiber 5.1g

Protein 13.2g

Cholesterol 15mg

Sodium 542mg

Calcium 216mg

Iron 2.2mg

1   (15-ounce) can Mexican-style stewed tomatoes, undrained
1   (15-ounce) can no-salt-added black beans, rinsed and drained
1   teaspoon ground cumin
Cooking spray
6   (6-inch) corn tortillas
1   cup (4 ounces) shredded Monterey Jack cheese
1   cup finely chopped tomato (about 1 large)
½   cup nonfat sour cream
1   tablespoon sliced green onions
1   tablespoon chopped fresh cilantro or parsley

1. Combine first 3 ingredients in a medium saucepan; bring to a boil. Reduce heat, and simmer 5 minutes. Spread one-third of bean mixture in a 2-quart microwave-safe dish coated with cooking spray. Arrange half of tortillas over bean mixture; top with ½ cup cheese. Repeat layers once; top with remaining one-third bean mixture.

2. Cover with heavy-duty plastic wrap, and vent. Microwave at HIGH 4 to 5 minutes or until cheese melts. Top with chopped tomato and remaining ingredients. Yield: 6 servings.

FOR A QUICK MEAL: Serve with a tomato-cucumber salad drizzled with fat-free Italian dressing and with a dish of apricot halves.

Seasoned Cannellini Beans

1	teaspoon olive oil
2	teaspoons bottled minced garlic
1	cup finely chopped celery
1	cup canned low-sodium vegetable broth
2	(15.5-ounce) cans cannellini beans, rinsed and drained
1	tablespoon finely chopped fresh sage or 1 teaspoon ground sage
¼	teaspoon pepper
¼	teaspoon salt
¼	cup coarsely chopped fresh flat-leaf parsley
¼	cup freshly grated Parmesan cheese

POINTS

3

EXCHANGES

1 Lean Meat

1½ Starch

PER SERVING

Calories 176

Carbohydrate 22.6g

Fat 4.2g (saturated 1.7g)

Fiber 4.0g

Protein 10.8g

Cholesterol 6mg

Sodium 514mg

Calcium 163mg

Iron 2.7mg

1. Heat oil in a large saucepan over medium-high heat. Add garlic and celery; cook 3 minutes or until tender, stirring often. Add broth and next 4 ingredients; bring to a boil. Reduce heat, and simmer, uncovered, 10 minutes.

2. Spoon into individual soup bowls, and sprinkle evenly with parsley and Parmesan cheese. Yield: 4 (1-cup) servings.

FOR A QUICK MEAL: Serve with a tossed green salad and toasted Italian bread. For extra flavor, lightly spray bread slices with olive oil-flavored cooking spray before toasting under the broiler until golden.

Fiesta Black Beans over Rice *(photo, page 42)*

POINTS

4

EXCHANGES

4 Starch

1 Vegetable

PER SERVING

Calories 309

Carbohydrate 66.4g

Fat 0.6g (saturated 0.1g)

Fiber 9.2g

Protein 10.4g

Cholesterol 0mg

Sodium 534mg

Calcium 115mg

Iron 4.6mg

2 family-size bags quick-cooking boil-in-bag rice, uncooked

Cooking spray

1¼ cups frozen chopped green pepper

1 cup frozen chopped onion

4 (15-ounce) cans no-salt-added black beans, drained

2 (14.5-ounce) cans no-salt-added diced tomatoes, undrained

1 (15-ounce) can chili-style stewed tomatoes

1¼ cups salsa

½ cup chopped fresh cilantro or parsley

1 teaspoon ground cumin

1. Cook rice according to package directions, omitting salt and fat.

2. While rice cooks, coat a Dutch oven with cooking spray. Place over medium-high heat until hot. Add pepper and onion; cook until crisp-tender, stirring often. Add beans and remaining 5 ingredients. Bring to a boil; reduce heat, and simmer, uncovered, 10 minutes, stirring occasionally.

3. Spoon rice into individual bowls; top evenly with bean mixture. Yield: 6 servings.

 FOR A QUICK MEAL: Serve with baked tortilla wedges and Citrus with Granola Crunch (page 186).

Potato Cakes with Chili Topping *(photo, page 63)*

1 (1-pound, 4-ounce) package refrigerated hash brown potatoes	**POINTS** 3
¼ cup fat-free egg substitute	
2 tablespoons all-purpose flour	
Cooking spray	**EXCHANGES**
1 (15-ounce) can no-salt-added red kidney beans, drained	1 Lean Meat
1 (14.5-ounce) can chili-style chunky tomatoes, undrained	3 Starch
2 teaspoons chili powder	1 Vegetable
½ cup (2 ounces) shredded reduced-fat Monterey Jack cheese	

PER SERVING

Calories 300

Carbohydrate 54.4g

Fat 3.1g (saturated 1.6g)

Fiber 15.3g

Protein 16.1g

Cholesterol 9mg

Sodium 771mg

Calcium 193mg

Iron 5.1mg

1. Combine first 3 ingredients in a medium bowl, stirring well. Shape mixture into 8 (3-inch) patties; place on a baking sheet coated with cooking spray. Coat patties with cooking spray. Bake patties at 400° for 15 minutes or until golden, turning once.

2. While patties cook, combine beans, tomatoes, and chili powder in a small saucepan; bring to a boil over medium-high heat, stirring often. Cover, reduce heat, and simmer 5 minutes.

3. Place 2 patties on each serving plate; spoon tomato mixture over patties, and sprinkle with cheese. Yield: 4 servings.

 FOR A QUICK MEAL: Serve with a simple tossed salad and cornbread.

Moroccan Vegetable Couscous

POINTS

6

EXCHANGES

4 Starch

1 Vegetable

½ Fruit

PER SERVING

Calories 366

Carbohydrate 73.0g

Fat 3.9g (saturated 0.3g)

Fiber 6.1g

Protein 13.4g

Cholesterol 0mg

Sodium 594mg

Calcium 73mg

Iron 3.6mg

2½ cups canned vegetable broth, divided
½ cup currants or raisins
1 teaspoon ground cumin
½ teaspoon ground allspice
⅛ teaspoon salt
1 (15.5-ounce) can garbanzo beans, drained
1 (10-ounce) package couscous, uncooked
1 teaspoon olive oil
2 medium carrots, scraped and thinly sliced
2 medium turnips, cut into quarters and thinly sliced

1. Combine 2 cups broth and next 5 ingredients in a saucepan; bring to a boil. Stir in couscous; cover tightly, and remove from heat. Let stand 5 minutes or until liquid is absorbed.

2. While couscous stands, pour oil into a large nonstick skillet; place over medium-high heat until hot. Add carrot and turnips; cook 3 minutes, stirring often. Add remaining ½ cup broth; cover, reduce heat, and simmer 3 to 4 minutes or until vegetables are tender.

3. Fluff couscous with a fork. Serve couscous topped with vegetable mixture. Yield: 5 servings.

> FOR A QUICK MEAL: Serve this easy entrée as a one-dish meal. Just cut pita bread into wedges, and toast them to put alongside the plates.

Couscous-Stuffed Peppers *(photo, page 62)*

1	(5.8-ounce) package roasted garlic- and olive oil-flavored couscous
3	small sweet yellow, red, or green peppers
1	cup chopped fresh spinach
⅓	cup grated Parmesan cheese
2	tablespoons slivered almonds, toasted
2	tablespoons sliced green onions

POINTS

6

EXCHANGES

1 Medium-Fat Meat

3 Starch

1 Vegetable

PER SERVING

Calories 338

Carbohydrate 51.4g

Fat 7.0g (saturated 2.0g)

Fiber 5.6g

Protein 13.3g

Cholesterol 7mg

Sodium 660mg

Calcium 156mg

Iron 3.0mg

1. Prepare couscous according to package directions, omitting fat.

2. Meanwhile, cut each pepper in half lengthwise; discard seeds and membranes.

3. Combine couscous, spinach, and cheese; spoon evenly into pepper halves. Place in a 2½-quart microwave-safe baking dish. Cover with heavy-duty plastic wrap, and vent. Microwave at HIGH 8 minutes or until peppers are tender. Sprinkle with almonds and green onions. Yield: 3 servings.

FOR A QUICK MEAL: Serve with Greek Vegetable Salad (page 183).

Herbed Alfredo Sauce over Pasta

POINTS

7

EXCHANGES

1 Lean Meat

4 Starch

PER SERVING

Calories 361

Carbohydrate 62.2g

Fat 4.0g (saturated 1.6g)

Fiber 3.1g

Protein 17.7g

Cholesterol 9mg

Sodium 363mg

Calcium 329mg

Iron 2.3mg

10 ounces roasted garlic- and red pepper-flavored angel hair pasta, uncooked

Cooking spray

¼ cup sliced green onions (about 2)

1 teaspoon minced garlic

2 tablespoons all-purpose flour

1 (12-ounce) can evaporated skimmed milk, divided

½ cup grated Parmesan cheese

¼ cup chopped fresh parsley or 1 tablespoon dried parsley

1 tablespoon chopped fresh basil or 1 teaspoon dried basil

¼ teaspoon salt

¼ teaspoon pepper

1. Cook pasta according to package directions, omitting salt and fat. Drain and set aside.

2. While pasta cooks, coat a medium saucepan with cooking spray; place over medium heat until hot. Add green onions and garlic; cook, stirring constantly, 2 minutes.

3. Combine flour and ⅓ cup milk, stirring until smooth. Add remaining milk, stirring well. Add to saucepan; cook over medium heat, stirring constantly, until thickened. Add cheese and remaining 4 ingredients; cook until thoroughly heated. Toss with pasta; serve immediately. Yield: 5 (1-cup) servings.

FOR A QUICK MEAL: Serve with steamed zucchini and warm French bread. For extra flavor, we used roasted garlic and red pepper angel hair pasta (by Skinner) to test this recipe. You can use 10 ounces of any pasta you have on hand.

Linguine with Vegetables and Asiago Cheese *(photo, page 43)*

8   ounces linguine or fettuccine, uncooked
¾   cup canned vegetable broth
1   (16-ounce) package fresh broccoli, cauliflower, carrot medley
½   (10-ounce) container light Alfredo sauce (such as Contadina)
½   cup grated Asiago or Parmesan cheese
Freshly ground pepper

POINTS

7

EXCHANGES

1 Medium-Fat Meat
3 Starch
2 Vegetable

PER SERVING

Calories 341
Carbohydrate 53.5g
Fat 6.9g (saturated 3.7g)
Fiber 4.4g
Protein 16.7g
Cholesterol 19mg
Sodium 550mg
Calcium 283mg
Iron 2.6mg

1. Cook pasta according to package directions, omitting fat and salt.

2. While pasta cooks, combine broth and vegetables in a medium saucepan over low heat. Cover and simmer 5 minutes or until vegetables are crisp-tender. Add Alfredo sauce, stirring well.

3. Drain pasta, and place in a serving bowl. Add vegetable mixture, and toss to coat; top with cheese, and sprinkle with pepper. Yield: 4 (1¾-cup) servings.

 FOR A QUICK MEAL: Serve with Caesar salad and crusty Italian rolls.

RECIPE TIME: 15 minutes

Creamy Macaroni and Cheese

POINTS

7

EXCHANGES
1 Medium-Fat Meat
3 Starch

PER SERVING
Calories 323
Carbohydrate 45.7g
Fat 7.8g (saturated 3.9g)
Fiber 1.0g
Protein 15.9g
Cholesterol 23mg
Sodium 675mg
Calcium 384mg
Iron 2.1mg

3   cups elbow macaroni, uncooked
1   (10¾-ounce) can 98% fat-free cream of mushroom soup
1   cup (4 ounces) loaf process cheese spread, shredded
1   (12-ounce) can evaporated skimmed milk
Butter-flavored cooking spray
½   cup (2 ounces) shredded reduced-fat sharp Cheddar cheese
      or Swiss cheese
¼   cup fine, dry breadcrumbs
½   teaspoon paprika

1. Cook macaroni according to package directions, omitting salt and fat; drain. (Do not rinse.)

2. While macaroni cooks, combine soup, cheese spread, and milk in a heavy saucepan over medium heat, stirring constantly until cheese spread melts. (Do not boil.)

3. Coat an 11- x 7- x 1½-inch microwave-safe baking dish with cooking spray. Add macaroni. Pour cheese spread mixture over macaroni, and stir gently. Sprinkle with shredded Cheddar cheese; top with breadcrumbs, and sprinkle with paprika. Lightly coat breadcrumbs with cooking spray. Microwave at HIGH, uncovered, 5 minutes. Let stand 2 minutes before serving. Yield: 6 servings.

 FOR A QUICK MEAL: Serve with steamed carrots and a broccoli salad.

Creamy Penne Primavera

10 ounces penne (short tubular pasta), uncooked

1 (16-ounce) package frozen Sugar Snap stir-fry vegetable blend

½ (8-ounce) tub light cream cheese (about ½ cup)

½ cup nonfat sour cream

3 tablespoons fat-free milk

1½ teaspoons salt-free herb-and-spice blend (such as Mrs. Dash)

½ teaspoon salt

¼ cup refrigerated shredded Parmesan cheese

POINTS

7

EXCHANGES

1 Medium-Fat Meat

3 Starch

1 Vegetable

PER SERVING

Calories 337

Carbohydrate 50.5g

Fat 6.3g (saturated 3.2g)

Fiber 1.8g

Protein 14.2g

Cholesterol 17mg

Sodium 497mg

Calcium 127mg

Iron 0.1mg

1. Cook pasta according to package directions, omitting salt and fat. Add vegetables to pasta the last 2 minutes of cooking. Drain; set aside.

2. While pasta drains, melt cream cheese in the same saucepan pasta was cooked in (pan will still be warm) over low heat; add sour cream, stirring until smooth. Add milk, stirring until smooth. Add spice blend and salt; stir well. Add pasta mixture, and toss well. Sprinkle with Parmesan cheese. Serve immediately. Yield: 5 (1½-cup) servings.

 FOR A QUICK MEAL: Serve with Asparagus Salad with Blue Cheese (page 183) and warm dinner rolls.

Tomato-Feta Pasta

POINTS

6

EXCHANGES

3 Starch

1 Vegetable

1 Fat

PER SERVING

Calories 307

Carbohydrate 53.9g

Fat 5.7g (saturated 2.5g)

Fiber 3.2g

Protein 10.3g

Cholesterol 13mg

Sodium 653mg

Calcium 104mg

Iron 2.6mg

8	ounces penne (short tubular pasta), uncooked
1	(14½-ounce) can pasta-style chunky tomatoes, undrained
2	tablespoons lemon juice
½	teaspoon dried oregano
2	cloves garlic, minced
1½	teaspoons olive oil
¼	teaspoon pepper
½	cup crumbled feta cheese

1. Cook pasta according to package directions, omitting salt and fat; drain well.

2. While pasta cooks, combine tomatoes and next 3 ingredients in a saucepan. Bring to a boil; cook 2 minutes.

3. Combine pasta, oil, and pepper in a serving bowl; add tomato mixture, and toss gently. Sprinkle with cheese, and serve immediately. Yield: 4 (1-cup) servings.

 FOR A QUICK MEAL: Serve with Zesty Asparagus (page 184) and a fruit sorbet.

Cheese Ravioli with Tomatoes and Peppers

1   (9-ounce) package refrigerated cheese-filled ravioli, uncooked
1   teaspoon olive oil
1   medium-size green pepper, cut into thin strips
1   medium onion, cut into thin strips
2   teaspoons minced garlic
3   cups chopped fresh tomato (2 medium)
¾   teaspoon freshly ground black pepper
1   cup loosely packed basil leaves, slivered

1. Cook pasta according to package directions.

2. While pasta cooks, heat oil in a large nonstick skillet over medium-high heat. Add green pepper, onion, and garlic; cook 3 minutes or until vegetables begin to wilt. Stir in tomato, and cook 2 additional minutes or until tomatoes are soft. Stir in ground pepper and basil; remove from heat.

3. Drain pasta, and place in a large serving bowl; pour sauce over pasta. Serve immediately. Yield: 3 (1½-cup) servings.

FOR A QUICK MEAL: Serve with warm Italian bread sprinkled with garlic powder. For dessert, prepare Chocolate-Berry Angel Cake (page 187).

POINTS

7

EXCHANGES

1 Medium-Fat Meat
3 Starch
1 Vegetable

PER SERVING

Calories 362
Carbohydrate 50.8g
Fat 11.2g (saturated 5.3g)
Fiber 6.3g
Protein 16.3g
Cholesterol 70mg
Sodium 356mg
Calcium 226mg
Iron 2.4mg

Vegetarian Peanut Pasta *(photo, page 64)*

POINTS

7

EXCHANGES

1 Medium-Fat Meat

3 Starch

1 Vegetable

PER SERVING

Calories 339

Carbohydrate 54.2g

Fat 8.1g (saturated 0.1g)

Fiber 4.3g

Protein 12.3g

Cholesterol 0mg

Sodium 398mg

Calcium 57mg

Iron 4.9mg

¼ cup plus 2 tablespoons reduced-fat peanut butter

¼ cup plus 1½ teaspoons water

3 tablespoons brown sugar

3 tablespoons low-sodium soy sauce

3 tablespoons rice vinegar

¼ to ½ teaspoon dried crushed red pepper

8 ounces spaghetti, uncooked

10 ounces fresh snow pea pods, trimmed

1 large carrot, shredded

1. Combine first 6 ingredients in a small saucepan. Cook over medium heat until mixture begins to boil, stirring often; remove from heat, and set sauce aside.

2. While sauce cooks, cook pasta according to package directions, omitting salt and fat; add snow peas to pasta the last 3 minutes of cooking time. Drain and place in a large serving bowl. Add carrot and sauce, tossing to coat. Yield: 5 servings.

FOR A QUICK MEAL: Serve with warmed bread rounds, fresh orange wedges, and sliced bananas. You can substitute 1½ cups broccoli flowerets for snow peas in this pasta recipe—just cook as directed in step two. For a bit of crunch, sprinkle each serving with 2 teaspoons chopped dry roasted peanuts.

Hearty Spaghetti

12 ounces spaghetti, uncooked

Cooking spray

1 teaspoon bottled minced garlic

1 (10-ounce) package frozen chopped onion

1 (8-ounce) package sliced fresh mushrooms

1 (14½-ounce) can no-salt-added stewed tomatoes, undrained

1 (6-ounce) can tomato paste

1 cup water

1 (12-ounce) package all-vegetable burger crumbles

¼ teaspoon salt

1 tablespoon dried Italian seasoning

POINTS

6

EXCHANGES

3½ Starch

2 Vegetable

PER SERVING

Calories 349

Carbohydrate 63.6g

Fat 1.6g (saturated 0.2g)

Fiber 6.3g

Protein 20.7g

Cholesterol 0mg

Sodium 396mg

Calcium 95mg

Iron 5.9mg

1. Cook pasta according to package directions, omitting salt and fat; drain and keep warm.

2. While pasta cooks, coat a Dutch oven with cooking spray; place over medium-high heat until hot. Add garlic, onion, and mushrooms; cook 5 minutes or until liquid is absorbed, stirring occasionally.

3. Reduce heat to medium; add tomatoes, tomato paste, and water. Cook 1 minute, stirring well. Add vegetable crumbles, salt, and Italian seasoning. Cover, reduce heat to medium-low, and simmer 10 minutes, stirring once. Serve over pasta. Yield: 6 servings.

FOR A QUICK MEAL: Serve with a romaine salad tossed with fresh apple slices and creamy reduced-fat Ranch-style dressing. Lightly spray slices of Italian bread with butter-flavored cooking spray and toast them until golden.

Meatless Chili

POINTS

4

EXCHANGES

2 Lean Meat

2 Starch

1 Vegetable

PER SERVING

Calories 291

Carbohydrate 34.7g

Fat 5.9g (saturated 0.5g)

Fiber 11.4g

Protein 22.1g

Cholesterol 0mg

Sodium 863mg

Calcium 86mg

Iron 3.0mg

Cooking spray

2　teaspoons minced garlic

1　large onion, chopped

1　(16-ounce) can chili hot beans, undrained

1　(14.5-ounce) can no-salt-added diced tomatoes, undrained

1　teaspoon chili powder

1　teaspoon ground cumin

12　ounces frozen vegetable and grain protein crumbles
　　(about 3 cups)

1. Coat a 4-quart saucepan with cooking spray. Place pan over medium-high heat until hot; add garlic and onion. Cook 3 minutes, stirring often. Add beans and next 3 ingredients. Bring to a boil, stirring occasionally; reduce heat, and simmer 5 minutes. Add protein crumbles, and cook 3 minutes. Yield: 4 (1½-cup) servings.

FOR A QUICK MEAL: Serve with crackers and a tossed salad. Or spoon some of the chili onto a warm flour tortilla, sprinkle with shredded lettuce and cheese, and roll up for a burrito.

Tomato-Feta Omelet
(recipe, page 38)

Couscous-Stuffed Peppers
(recipe, page 51)

Potato Cakes with Chili Topping
(recipe, page 49)

Vegetarian Peanut Pasta
(recipe, page 58)

meats

Burgers with Purple Onion Salsa

POINTS

4

EXCHANGES

2 Medium-Fat Meat

1 Vegetable

PER SERVING

Calories 181

Carbohydrate 8.2g

Fat 10.1g (saturated 3.7g)

Fiber 2.4g

Protein 16.4g

Cholesterol 46mg

Sodium 64mg

Calcium 23mg

Iron 2.1mg

1   pound ground round
1   large purple onion, finely chopped and divided (about 1½ cups)
2   tablespoons chili powder
Cooking spray
1   large tomato, chopped (about 1¾ cups)
1   teaspoon chili powder
2   tablespoons lime juice

1. Combine ground round, 2 tablespoons onion, and 2 tablespoons chili powder; shape into 6 (½-inch-thick) patties.

2. Coat a large nonstick skillet with cooking spray; place over medium-high heat until hot. Add patties, and cook 4 minutes on each side or until done.

3. While burgers cook, combine remaining onion, tomato, 1 teaspoon chili powder, and lime juice; spoon over cooked burgers. Yield: 6 servings.

 FOR A QUICK MEAL: Serve with sliced cucumbers and reduced-fat potato chips.

Sante Fe Skillet Hamburger Casserole

1   pound ground round
¾   cup chopped onion
¾   cup chopped green pepper
1½   cups instant rice, uncooked (such as Uncle Ben's 5-minute
        rice)
1½   cups canned no-salt-added beef broth
¼   teaspoon salt
¼   teaspoon pepper
1   (14½-ounce) can Mexican-style stewed tomatoes, undrained
¾   cup (3 ounces) shredded reduced-fat sharp Cheddar cheese

POINTS

8

EXCHANGES

3 Medium-Fat Meat

1½ Starch

1 Vegetable

PER SERVING

Calories 346

Carbohydrate 28.5g

Fat 15.8g (saturated 6.8g)

Fiber 2.1g

Protein 21.1g

Cholesterol 62mg

Sodium 488mg

Calcium 152mg

Iron 2.9mg

1. Combine first 3 ingredients in a large nonstick skillet; cook over medium-high heat until beef is browned and vegetables are tender, stirring until beef crumbles. (Do not drain.)

2. Add rice and next 4 ingredients. Cover, reduce heat, and simmer 5 minutes or until rice is tender and liquid is absorbed. Sprinkle with cheese; serve immediately. Yield: 6 servings.

 FOR A QUICK MEAL: Serve with steamed green beans and Apple Pie Sundae (page 186).

Spaghetti with Beef, Tomatoes, and Zucchini

POINTS

7

EXCHANGES

2 Lean Meat

2 Starch

2 Vegetable

PER SERVING

Calories 332

Carbohydrate 46.4g

Fat 7.9g (saturated 2.9g)

Fiber 2.2g

Protein 19.3g

Cholesterol 35mg

Sodium 336mg

Calcium 33mg

Iron 3.7mg

1 (7-ounce) package thin spaghetti

½ pound lean ground round

¼ cup chopped onion

2 (8-ounce) cans no-salt-added tomato sauce

1 teaspoon dried Italian seasoning

½ teaspoon salt

¼ teaspoon garlic powder

¼ teaspoon dried crushed red pepper

1½ cups coarsely chopped zucchini (about 1 medium)

1½ cups coarsely chopped tomato (about 1 medium)

1. Cook spaghetti according to package directions, omitting salt and fat.

2. While spaghetti cooks, cook ground round and onion in a large nonstick skillet over high heat 4 to 5 minutes or until beef is browned, stirring until beef crumbles. Drain beef mixture, if necessary; wipe skillet with paper towels. Return beef mixture to skillet. Stir in tomato sauce and next 4 ingredients. Cook over medium heat 2 to 4 minutes or until hot and bubbly, stirring occasionally.

3. Stir in cooked spaghetti and zucchini. Cook 2 minutes, stirring occasionally. Stir in tomato. Yield: 4 (1½-cup) servings.

 FOR A QUICK MEAL: Serve with Sliced Melon with Raspberry Sauce (page 182) and fat-free lemon frozen yogurt.

South-of-the-Border Pizzas *(photo, page 81)*

3 (10-inch) flour tortillas
½ pound ground round
1 (15-ounce) can no-salt-added black beans, rinsed and drained
1 (1.25-ounce) package reduced-sodium taco seasoning
¼ cup water
2 large tomatoes, finely chopped
½ cup sliced green onions
2 tablespoons chopped fresh cilantro
1 tablespoon minced jalapeño pepper
1 cup shredded reduced-fat Mexican cheese blend

POINTS

5

EXCHANGES

3 Lean Meat

1 ½ Starch

1 Vegetable

PER SERVING

Calories 300

Carbohydrate 40.4g

Fat 7.6g (saturated 3.2g)

Fiber 6.2g

Protein 21.6g

Cholesterol 30mg

Sodium 641mg

Calcium 227mg

Iron 3.0mg

1. Place tortillas on two baking sheets, and bake at 450° for 2 minutes or until slightly crisp.

2. While tortillas bake, cook ground round in a nonstick skillet over medium heat until browned, stirring until it crumbles. Drain and pat dry with paper towels; return to skillet. Add beans, taco seasoning, and water; bring to a boil. Reduce heat to low, and simmer 3 minutes, stirring often.

3. Spread beef mixture over tortillas, leaving a ½-inch border. Combine tomato and next 3 ingredients; sprinkle over beef mixture. Top with cheese.

4. Bake at 450° for 4 minutes or until cheese melts and tortillas are lightly browned. Remove pizzas to a cutting board; let stand 5 minutes before cutting into wedges. Yield: 6 servings.

FOR A QUICK MEAL: Serve with a tossed green salad drizzled with fat-free Italian dressing. For dessert, serve fresh pineapple slices.

Chipotle Chili con Carne

POINTS

5

EXCHANGES

2 Lean Meat

2 Starch

1 Vegetable

PER SERVING

Calories 265

Carbohydrate 33.6g

Fat 8.7g (saturated 3.0g)

Fiber 7.1g

Protein 22.0g

Cholesterol 38mg

Sodium 682mg

Calcium 43mg

Iron 2.3mg

½   pound extra-lean ground beef
1   small green pepper, chopped
1   teaspoon fresh or bottled minced garlic
1   (16-ounce) can spicy chili beans in sauce, undrained
1   (14½-ounce) can no-salt-added stewed tomatoes, undrained
1   to 2 teaspoons minced canned chipotle peppers in adobo
    sauce
¼   cup nonfat sour cream
¼   cup chopped fresh cilantro or parsley (optional)

1. Cook ground beef in a large saucepan over medium heat until browned, stirring until it crumbles. Drain and pat dry with paper towels; wipe drippings from pan with a paper towel. Return beef to pan. Add green pepper and garlic; cook 1 minute.

2. Add beans, tomatoes, and chipotle pepper; bring to a boil over high heat. Cover, reduce heat, and simmer 15 minutes, stirring occasionally. Top each serving with sour cream. Sprinkle with cilantro, if desired. Yield: 4 servings.

Note: You can refrigerate leftover canned chipotle peppers up to one week or freeze up to three months. Enjoy them brushed on grilled beef or pork, or mix 1 to 2 teaspoons with fat-free mayonnaise or sour cream for a spicy sandwich spread or potato topper.

 FOR A QUICK MEAL: Serve with warm corn muffins and Cinnamon-Spiced Bananas (page 186).

Hamburger-Noodle Skillet

1	pound extra-lean ground beef
1	(10-ounce) package frozen chopped onion, celery, and pepper seasoning blend
1½	cups water
1	(10¾-ounce) can reduced-fat, reduced-sodium tomato soup
1	(8-ounce) can no-salt-added tomato sauce
½	(8-ounce) package medium egg noodles
¼	teaspoon garlic powder
1	(8¾-ounce) can whole-kernel corn, rinsed and drained
1	(2.25-ounce) can sliced ripe olives, drained
1	cup (4 ounces) shredded reduced-fat sharp Cheddar cheese

POINTS

8

EXCHANGES

2 Medium-Fat Meat

2 Starch

1 Vegetable

PER SERVING

Calories 361

Carbohydrate 33.9g

Fat 15.8g (saturated 6.5g)

Fiber 1.4g

Protein 21.2g

Cholesterol 70mg

Sodium 549mg

Calcium 187mg

Iron 2.5mg

1. Cook ground beef and frozen seasoning blend in a large non-stick skillet over medium-high heat until beef is browned, stirring until it crumbles. Drain and pat dry; return mixture to skillet.

2. Add water and next 4 ingredients to beef mixture; bring to a boil. Reduce heat; simmer 9 to 11 minutes or until noodles are tender. Add corn and olives, stirring well; cook until thoroughly heated. Sprinkle with cheese. Serve immediately. Yield: 6 servings.

 FOR A QUICK MEAL: Serve with a tossed green salad and toasted Boboli breadsticks.

Beef Fajitas *(photo, cover)*

POINTS

6

EXCHANGES

2 Lean Meat

2 Starch

1 Vegetable

PER SERVING

Calories 317

Carbohydrate 38.6g

Fat 9.3g (saturated 3.8g)

Fiber 3.4g

Protein 19.7g

Cholesterol 41mg

Sodium 697mg

Calcium 24mg

Iron 2.7mg

1   pound lean flank steak

Cooking spray

½   cup bottled chili sauce

1   tablespoon no-salt-added Creole seasoning

3   cups onion strips

3   cups sweet red pepper strips

6   (8-inch) fat-free flour tortillas

Fresh cilantro sprigs (optional)

1. Cut steak diagonally across the grain into ¼-inch-thick slices. Coat a large nonstick skillet with cooking spray, and place over medium-high heat until hot. Add steak, chili sauce, and Creole seasoning; cook 4 minutes or until meat is done. Remove from skillet, and set aside. Wipe skillet clean with a paper towel.

2. Coat skillet with cooking spray; place over medium-high heat until hot. Add onion and red pepper, and cook 7 minutes or until tender, stirring often.

3. Wrap tortillas in wax paper; microwave at HIGH 30 seconds. Spoon steak and vegetable mixture over warm tortillas; wrap or fold tortillas around mixture. Garnish with cilantro sprigs, if desired. Serve immediately. Yield: 6 servings.

 FOR A QUICK MEAL: Serve with warm black beans sprinkled with shredded reduced-fat Monterey Jack cheese.

Mexican-Style Steak and Beans

1 (1-pound) lean flank steak (½ inch thick)
Cooking spray
1 tablespoon mild Mexican seasoning blend (such as Morton & Bassett)
½ teaspoon salt
2 small green peppers, cut into thin strips
1 cup frozen chopped onion
1 (10-ounce) can diced tomatoes and green chiles, undrained
1 (15-ounce) can no-salt-added pinto beans, rinsed and drained
3 cups hot cooked rice

POINTS
6

EXCHANGES
2 Lean Meat
2 Starch
2 Vegetable

PER SERVING
Calories 335
Carbohydrate 41.8g
Fat 7.6g (saturated 3.1g)
Fiber 5.5g
Protein 21.7g
Cholesterol 38mg
Sodium 461mg
Calcium 69mg
Iron 3.8mg

1. Cut steak into 6 even pieces. Place in a 3½- to 4-quart electric slow cooker coated with cooking spray. Sprinkle steak with Mexican seasoning blend and salt. Add green peppers, onion, and tomatoes and green chiles. Cover and cook on HIGH heat 4 hours, adding pinto beans during the last 30 minutes of cooking. Serve over rice. Yield: 6 servings.

FOR A QUICK MEAL: Serve with warm flour tortillas and a romaine salad that's drizzled with fat-free Ranch-style dressing.

Barbecued Steak Pizza

POINTS

7

EXCHANGES

3 Lean Meat

1 Starch

1 Vegetable

PER SERVING

Calories 291

Carbohydrate 23.3g

Fat 9.5g (saturated 2.8g)

Fiber 0.4g

Protein 27.3g

Cholesterol 64mg

Sodium 520mg

Calcium 96mg

Iron 2.4mg

Cooking spray

1   pound lean boneless top sirloin steak

½   cup barbecue sauce

1   (10-ounce) package Italian bread shell (such as Boboli)

½   cup onion strips

½   cup green pepper strips

½   cup low-fat shredded Cheddar cheese

1. Coat grill rack with cooking spray; place on grill over medium-hot coals (350° to 400°). Brush both sides of steak with barbecue sauce. Brush remaining sauce over bread shell. Place steak on rack; grill, uncovered, 5 to 6 minutes on each side or to desired degree of doneness.

2. While steak grills, coat a large nonstick skillet with cooking spray; place over medium-high heat until hot. Add onion and pepper; cook 3 minutes or until crisp-tender, stirring often. Spoon vegetables over bread shell.

3. Arrange beef in a spiral pattern over vegetables, and sprinkle with cheese. Broil 3 to 4 minutes or until cheese melts. Yield: 6 servings.

FOR A QUICK MEAL: Serve with a salad made of fresh spinach, sliced purple onion, and mandarin orange sections; drizzle fat-free poppy seed dressing over the salad.

Chuckwagon Steak with Chili Rub

1   pound lean boneless sirloin steak (about ½ inch thick)
Cooking spray
1   tablespoon chili powder
2   teaspoons coarsely ground pepper
½   teaspoon salt
4   cloves garlic, minced

1. Coat both sides of steak with cooking spray. Combine chili powder and remaining 3 ingredients; rub on both sides of steak.

2. Coat grill rack with cooking spray; place on grill over medium-hot coals (350° to 400°). Place steak on rack; grill, covered, 5 minutes on each side or to desired degree of doneness. Yield: 4 servings.

POINTS
4

EXCHANGES
3 Lean Meat

PER SERVING
Calories 189
Carbohydrate 2.7g
Fat 7.0g (saturated 2.6g)
Fiber 1.0g
Protein 27.7g
Cholesterol 80mg
Sodium 372mg
Calcium 25mg
Iron 3.6mg

FOR A QUICK MEAL: Serve with steamed Sugar Snap peas and an endive salad. Dress up the endive with a splash of balsamic vinegar and a sprinkling of crumbled blue cheese.

Chili-Rubbed Sirloin with Corn-Bean Salsa

POINTS

5

EXCHANGES

3 Lean Meat

1½ Starch

PER SERVING

Calories 283

Carbohydrate 22.6g

Fat 7.5g (saturated 2.6g)

Fiber 4.0g

Protein 32.4g

Cholesterol 80mg

Sodium 240mg

Calcium 38mg

Iron 4.2mg

1   tablespoon chili powder
1   teaspoon ground cumin
½   teaspoon ground red pepper
1   (1-pound) lean boneless top sirloin steak (1 inch thick)
Cooking spray
½   cup thick and chunky cilantro-flavored salsa
1   cup frozen whole-kernel corn, thawed
1   cup drained canned no-salt-added pinto beans
½   cup sliced green onions

1. Combine first 3 ingredients in a small bowl; rub evenly over steak, pressing onto steak.

2. Coat grill rack with cooking spray; place on grill over hot coals (400° to 500°). Place steak on rack; grill, covered, 6 minutes on each side or to desired degree of doneness.

3. While steak grills, combine salsa and remaining 3 ingredients.

4. Slice steak diagonally across grain into ¼-inch-thick slices. Top with salsa mixture. Yield: 4 servings.

FOR A QUICK MEAL: Serve with a tossed green salad. For dessert, serve Melon Boat with Frozen Yogurt (page 186).

Thyme-Scented Tenderloin Steaks *(photo, page 82)*

2 teaspoons dried thyme

2 teaspoons bottled minced garlic or 4 cloves garlic, minced

¼ teaspoon salt

¼ teaspoon freshly ground pepper

4 (4-ounce) beef tenderloin steaks (¾ inch thick)

Cooking spray

1. Combine first 4 ingredients in a small bowl, and rub on both sides of steaks.

2. Coat a 10-inch cast-iron skillet with cooking spray; place over medium heat until hot. Add steaks; cook 4 to 6 minutes on each side or to desired degree of doneness. Yield: 4 servings.

 FOR A QUICK MEAL: Serve with parslied noodles and Mushroom and Pepper Skillet (page 185).

POINTS

4

EXCHANGES

3 Lean Meat

PER SERVING

Calories 174

Carbohydrate 1.0g

Fat 7.6g (saturated 3.0g)

Fiber 0.2g

Protein 23.7g

Cholesterol 70mg

Sodium 208mg

Calcium 23mg

Iron 4.1mg

Grilled Veal Chops with Greens

POINTS

4

EXCHANGES

3 Lean Meat

1 Vegetable

PER SERVING

Calories 205

Carbohydrate 5.1g

Fat 7.2g (saturated 1.8g)

Fiber 1.3g

Protein 29.1g

Cholesterol 101mg

Sodium 97mg

Calcium 58mg

Iron 2.0mg

2   tablespoons lemon juice, divided

1   teaspoon olive oil

½   teaspoon pepper, divided

8   cups packaged European-style Italian salad greens (romaine, radicchio, and endive)

¼   teaspoon garlic powder

½   teaspoon dried rosemary

4   (6-ounce) lean center-cut loin veal chops (½ inch thick)

Cooking spray

1. Combine 1 tablespoon lemon juice, oil, and ¼ teaspoon pepper in a large bowl, stirring well. Add salad greens, and toss to coat.

2. Combine remaining 1 tablespoon lemon juice, remaining ¼ teaspoon pepper, garlic powder, and rosemary in a bowl; rub mixture over veal.

3. Coat grill rack with cooking spray; place on grill over hot coals (400° to 500°). Place veal on rack; grill, covered, 3 to 4 minutes on each side or until done. Serve veal topped with greens mixture. Yield: 4 servings.

 FOR A QUICK MEAL: Serve with steamed new potatoes. For dessert, serve Strawberry-Amaretto Smoothie (page 187).

Veal Marsala *(photo, page 83)*

Cooking spray
1   (8-ounce) package sliced fresh mushrooms
¼   cup all-purpose flour
¼   teaspoon salt
⅛   teaspoon cracked black pepper
½   pound veal scaloppine or very thin veal cutlets
1½   teaspoons margarine
½   cup Marsala

1. Coat a large nonstick skillet with cooking spray; place skillet over medium-high heat until hot. Add mushrooms, and cook 5 minutes or until tender. Set aside; keep warm.

2. While mushrooms cook, place flour, salt, and pepper in a large heavy-duty, zip-top plastic bag. Seal bag; shake to mix. Add veal; seal bag, and shake to coat veal. Remove veal from flour mixture, reserving 1 tablespoon flour mixture; discard remaining flour mixture.

3. Melt margarine in skillet over medium-high heat. Add veal, and cook 3 minutes on each side or until browned. Transfer veal to a serving platter, and keep warm.

4. Combine wine and reserved 1 tablespoon flour, stirring well with a wire whisk; add to skillet. Bring to a boil, scraping browned particles that cling to bottom of skillet. Spoon mushroom mixture and wine mixture over veal. Yield: 2 servings.

FOR A QUICK MEAL: Serve with steamed fresh snow pea pods.

POINTS
5

EXCHANGES
3 Lean Meat
1 Starch
1 Vegetable

PER SERVING
Calories 253
Carbohydrate 19.7g
Fat 7.0g (saturated 1.6g)
Fiber 1.9g
Protein 27.0g
Cholesterol 94mg
Sodium 434mg
Calcium 32mg
Iron 3.3mg

Lamb Chops with Honey-Balsamic Glaze

POINTS

6

EXCHANGES

4 Lean Meat

½ Starch

PER SERVING

Calories 270

Carbohydrate 6.2g

Fat 11.1g (saturated 3.9g)

Fiber 0.0g

Protein 33.7g

Cholesterol 106mg

Sodium 97mg

Calcium 23mg

Iron 2.4mg

4   (5-ounce) lean lamb loin chops

Cooking spray

¾   cup canned no-salt-added beef broth

¼   cup dry red wine

2   tablespoons balsamic vinegar

1   tablespoon honey

2   teaspoons cornstarch

1   tablespoon minced fresh mint

1. Coat both sides of lamb chops with cooking spray. Place a large nonstick skillet over medium-high heat until hot; add lamb, and cook 5 minutes on each side.

2. Combine broth and next 4 ingredients, stirring until smooth; add to lamb in skillet, stirring well. Cook lamb in glaze 3 minutes on each side or to desired degree of doneness, stirring glaze often. Transfer lamb to a serving platter. Stir mint into glaze. Pour over lamb, and serve immediately. Yield: 4 servings.

 FOR A QUICK MEAL: Serve with herbed orzo and Zesty Asparagus (page 184).

South-of-the-Border Pizzas
(recipe, page 69)

Thyme-Scented
Tenderloin Steak
(recipe, page 77)

Veal Marsala
(recipe, page 79)

Mint-Grilled Lamb Chops *(photo, facing page)*

⅓   cup fresh mint leaves, chopped
2   tablespoons plain low-fat yogurt
2   cloves garlic, crushed
4   (5-ounce) lean lamb loin chops (1 inch thick)
1   small lemon, cut in half
Cooking spray
Fresh mint sprigs (optional)

1. Combine first 3 ingredients in a small bowl.

2. Trim fat from lamb. Rub lemon halves on both sides of lamb. Coat grill rack with cooking spray; place on grill over medium-hot coals (350° to 400°). Place lamb on rack; grill, covered, 5 minutes. Turn lamb; spread mint mixture evenly over lamb. Cook 5 additional minutes or to desired degree of doneness. Garnish with mint sprigs, if desired. Yield: 4 servings.

POINTS

4

EXCHANGES

3 Lean Meat

PER SERVING

Calories 173
Carbohydrate 1.2g
Fat 7.9g (saturated 2.9g)
Fiber 0.1g
Protein 23.0g
Cholesterol 74mg
Sodium 66mg
Calcium 32mg
Iron 1.7mg

 FOR A QUICK MEAL: Serve with couscous and Maple-Glazed Carrots (page 184).

Peppered Lamb Chops

POINTS

4

EXCHANGES

3 Lean Meat

PER SERVING

Calories 181

Carbohydrate 1.4g

Fat 8.0g (saturated 2.8g)

Fiber 0.3g

Protein 24.1g

Cholesterol 76mg

Sodium 179mg

Calcium 22mg

Iron 1.9mg

1   tablespoon Dijon mustard

2   teaspoons minced garlic

2   teaspoons coarsely ground pepper

4   (5-ounce) lean lamb loin chops (1½ inch thick)

1. Combine first 3 ingredients; brush over both sides of lamb. Broil 5½ inches from heat 9 minutes on each side or to desired degree of doneness. Yield: 4 servings.

 FOR A QUICK MEAL: Serve with saffron rice and Parmesan Broiled Tomatoes (page 185).

Simmered Lamb and Peppers

2   small sweet red peppers, cut into thin strips (about 2 cups)

1   small onion, vertically sliced (about 1 cup)

Cooking spray

4   (5-ounce) lean lamb loin chops

½   cup dry red wine

1   teaspoon instant beef-flavored bouillon granules

¼   teaspoon garlic powder

⅛   teaspoon pepper

POINTS

4

EXCHANGES

3 Lean Meat

1 Vegetable

PER SERVING

Calories 187

Carbohydrate 5.3g

Fat 7.1g (saturated 2.5g)

Fiber 1.3g

Protein 24.2g

Cholesterol 74mg

Sodium 316mg

Calcium 23mg

Iron 2.9mg

1. Coat red pepper and onion with cooking spray. Place a large nonstick skillet over medium-high heat until hot. Add red pepper and onion; stir-fry 2 minutes. Remove from skillet, and set aside. Coat both sides of lamb with cooking spray; add lamb to skillet, and cook 3 minutes on each side.

2. Combine wine and remaining 3 ingredients, stirring well. Pour over lamb; bring to a boil over medium-high heat. Cook 6 minutes or to desired degree of doneness, turning lamb once and stirring occasionally.

3. Transfer lamb to a serving platter. Stir vegetables into wine mixture; cook until thoroughly heated, stirring occasionally. Spoon vegetables over lamb. Yield: 4 servings.

 FOR A QUICK MEAL: Serve with Greek Rice (page 185) and warm focaccia.

Tangy Raspberry Lamb Kabobs

POINTS
6

EXCHANGES
4 Lean Meat
½ Starch

PER SERVING
Calories 258
Carbohydrate 6.7g
Fat 10.6g (saturated 3.7g)
Fiber 0.0g
Protein 31.9g
Cholesterol 101mg
Sodium 118mg
Calcium 21mg
Iron 2.2mg

¼ cup seedless raspberry jam
¼ cup balsamic vinegar
1   teaspoon Dijon mustard
½ teaspoon crumbled dried rosemary
1¼ pounds lean boneless leg of lamb, cut into 1-inch pieces
Cooking spray

1. Combine first 4 ingredients in a bowl. Add lamb, tossing to coat. Thread lamb onto four 6-inch skewers, leaving space between pieces. Brush kabobs with jam mixture.

2. Coat grill rack with cooking spray; place on grill over medium-hot coals (350° to 400°). Place kabobs on rack; grill, covered, 3 to 4 minutes. Turn kabobs, and brush with jam mixture. Grill, covered, 3 to 4 additional minutes or to desired degree of doneness. Yield: 4 servings.

FOR A QUICK MEAL: Serve with rice, and accompany with grilled onions or mushrooms. For the onions, toss thickly sliced purple onion rings in jam mixture, and grill alongside kabobs. Or toss fresh mushrooms in jam mixture, and thread onto additional skewers.

Speedy Pork and Pepper

6   ounces linguine, uncooked
4   (4-ounce) boneless pork loin chops
2   teaspoons dried Italian seasoning
½   teaspoon salt
¼   teaspoon freshly ground pepper
Cooking spray
1½   cups chopped green pepper
1½   cups pasta sauce with garlic and herbs (such as Healthy
       Choice)

1. Cook pasta according to package directions, omitting salt and fat.

2. While pasta cooks, cut pork chops into thin strips. Combine Italian seasoning, salt, and ground pepper; sprinkle over pork, and toss well.

3. Coat a large nonstick skillet with cooking spray; place over medium-high heat until hot. Add pork mixture and green pepper; stir-fry 5 minutes or until pork is done and pepper is crisp-tender. Stir in pasta sauce, and cook until thoroughly heated; spoon over pasta. Serve immediately. Yield: 4 servings.

 FOR A QUICK MEAL: Serve with crisp breadsticks and fresh fruit salad.

POINTS

8

EXCHANGES

3 Lean Meat
2 Starch
2 Vegetable

PER SERVING

Calories 391
Carbohydrate 42.9g
Fat 9.7g (saturated 3.1g)
Fiber 3.6g
Protein 31.0g
Cholesterol 68mg
Sodium 663mg
Calcium 41mg
Iron 4.2mg

Pork Chops with Spiced Peach-Raisin Sauce

POINTS

6

EXCHANGES

3 Lean Meat

1½ Fruit

PER SERVING

Calories 283

Carbohydrate 26.5g

Fat 8.3g (saturated 3.0g)

Fiber 1.6g

Protein 25.9g

Cholesterol 71mg

Sodium 276mg

Calcium 17mg

Iron 1.5mg

1   (16-ounce) can sliced peaches in extra-light syrup, undrained

½   cup raisins

¾   cup orange juice

½   teaspoon ground nutmeg

¼   teaspoon ground ginger

Cooking spray

6   (4-ounce) boneless center-cut pork loin chops

½   teaspoon salt

2   tablespoons cornstarch

¼   cup water

1. Drain peaches, reserving syrup; set peaches aside. Combine syrup, raisins, and next 3 ingredients; set aside.

2. Coat a large nonstick skillet with cooking spray; place over medium-high heat until hot. Sprinkle pork with salt, and add to skillet; cook 4 minutes on each side or until browned. Reduce heat to medium. Add peaches and syrup mixture; cover and cook 5 minutes or until pork is done. Remove pork from skillet; set aside.

3. Combine cornstarch and water; add to skillet. Cook, stirring constantly, until mixture is thickened. Return pork to skillet, turning to coat with peach mixture. Yield: 6 servings.

 FOR A QUICK MEAL: Serve with couscous and a tossed green salad.

Pork Medaillons with Pear Sauce

4 (4-ounce) boneless center-cut pork loin chops (½ inch thick)
½ teaspoon pepper
¼ teaspoon salt
1 teaspoon margarine
2 firm, ripe pears
1 tablespoon sugar
½ teaspoon dried rosemary, crushed
½ cup unsweetened apple juice

POINTS
6

EXCHANGES
3 Lean Meat
1 ½ Fruit

PER SERVING
Calories 279
Carbohydrate 23.1g
Fat 9.5g (saturated 3.0g)
Fiber 2.7g
Protein 25.4g
Cholesterol 71mg
Sodium 234mg
Calcium 23mg
Iron 1.4mg

1. Sprinkle both sides of pork with pepper and salt. Melt margarine in a large nonstick skillet over medium-high heat. Add pork; cook 3 minutes on each side or until browned. Remove from skillet; set aside.

2. While pork cooks, core pears, and cut into ½-inch slices. Add pear slices to skillet; sprinkle with sugar and rosemary. Cook over medium-low heat 3 minutes, stirring often.

3. Pour apple juice into skillet; return pork to skillet. Simmer 6 to 8 minutes or until pork is done. Yield: 4 servings.

 FOR A QUICK MEAL: Serve with Rosemary Potatoes (page 185) and steamed zucchini.

Mediterranean Pork Chops

POINTS

6

EXCHANGES

3 Lean Meat

½ Starch

PER SERVING

Calories 247

Carbohydrate 9.7g

Fat 9.2g (saturated 3.1g)

Fiber 0.5g

Protein 29.7g

Cholesterol 82mg

Sodium 205mg

Calcium 124mg

Iron 1.1mg

2   teaspoons chopped fresh mint
2   teaspoons sugar
1   (8-ounce) carton plain nonfat yogurt
1½ tablespoons hoisin sauce
2   teaspoons curry powder
4   (4-ounce) boneless center-cut pork loin chops (½ inch thick), trimmed
Cooking spray

1. Combine mint and sugar in a small bowl, pressing mint into sugar with back of a spoon until blended. Stir in yogurt. Set aside.

2. Combine hoisin sauce and curry powder, stirring well; spread evenly on both sides of pork.

3. Coat grill rack with cooking spray; place on grill over medium-hot coals (350° to 400°). Place pork on rack; grill, covered, 5 minutes or until done, turning once. Serve pork with yogurt mixture. Yield: 4 servings.

 FOR A QUICK MEAL: Serve with Blue Cheese Green Beans (page 184) and warm dinner rolls.

Rum-Marinated Pork Chops

1   large onion, coarsely chopped (about 1½ cups)
½   teaspoon garlic powder
½   teaspoon dried crushed red pepper
½   teaspoon dried thyme
½   teaspoon ground cinnamon
⅛   teaspoon ground nutmeg
¼   cup dark rum
2   tablespoons lemon juice
4   (5-ounce) lean center-cut pork loin chops (½ inch thick),
     trimmed
Cooking spray

1. Combine first 6 ingredients in a large shallow dish. Stir in rum and lemon juice. Add pork, and turn to coat. Cover and marinate in refrigerator at least 8 hours. (You can marinate chops in a heavy-duty, zip-top plastic bag, if desired, turning bag several times to coat chops with marinade.) Remove chops from marinade, discarding marinade.

2. Coat grill rack with cooking spray; place on grill over medium-hot coals (350° to 400°). Place pork chops on rack; grill, covered, 10 minutes or until done, turning once. Yield: 4 servings.

FOR A QUICK MEAL: Serve with Minted Peas (page 185) and sliced tomatoes.

POINTS
5

EXCHANGES
3 Lean Meat
1 Vegetable

PER SERVING
Calories 206
Carbohydrate 3.1g
Fat 8.9g (saturated 3.1g)
Fiber 0.5g
Protein 27.1g
Cholesterol 82mg
Sodium 66mg
Calcium 16mg
Iron 1.1mg

Cumin-Rubbed Pork Chops *(photo, page 3)*

POINTS

6

EXCHANGES

4 Lean Meat

1 Starch

½ Fruit

PER SERVING

Calories 315

Carbohydrate 25.7g

Fat 9.6g (saturated 3.1g)

Fiber 4.0g

Protein 32.2g

Cholesterol 80mg

Sodium 434mg

Calcium 48mg

Iron 3.1mg

Cooking spray

4   (4-ounce) boneless center-cut pork loin chops

2   teaspoons ground cumin

¼   teaspoon salt

1   cup peeled, diced mango or papaya

1   cup rinsed and drained canned black beans

⅓   cup thick and chunky salsa

¼   cup chopped fresh cilantro or parsley

1. Coat grill rack with cooking spray; place on grill over medium-hot coals (350° to 400°). Sprinkle both sides of pork with cumin and salt; coat pork with cooking spray. Place pork on rack; grill, covered, 5 minutes on each side or until done.

2. While pork grills, combine mango, beans, and salsa in a small bowl; toss gently to coat. Serve with pork chops; sprinkle with cilantro. Yield: 4 servings.

FOR A QUICK MEAL: Serve with a tossed green salad drizzled with fat-free Ranch-style dressing and with warm cornbread sticks.

Salsa Pork Chops

1   cup medium or hot thick and chunky salsa
1   (15-ounce) can crushed pineapple in juice, undrained
½   cup chopped green onions
Cooking spray
4   (5-ounce) center-cut pork loin chops, trimmed

1. Combine first 3 ingredients in a bowl; set aside.

2. Coat a large nonstick skillet with cooking spray; place over medium-high heat until hot. Add pork, and cook 4 minutes on each side or until browned. Add salsa mixture to skillet; simmer, uncovered, 8 minutes or until pork is done, turning pork occasionally. Yield: 4 servings.

 FOR A QUICK MEAL: Serve with Creamy Corn Salad (page 183) and warm sourdough bread.

POINTS
6

EXCHANGES
3 Lean Meat
1 Vegetable
1 Fruit

PER SERVING
Calories 272
Carbohydrate 21.6g
Fat 8.7g (saturated 2.9g)
Fiber 2.1g
Protein 27.1g
Cholesterol 73mg
Sodium 361mg
Calcium 49mg
Iron 2.0mg

Szechuan Barbecue Pork

POINTS

6

EXCHANGES

2 Lean Meat

2½ Starch

2 Vegetable

PER SERVING

Calories 336

Carbohydrate 48.1g

Fat 3.7g (saturated 1.2g)

Fiber 3.2g

Protein 23.9g

Cholesterol 62mg

Sodium 564mg

Calcium 51mg

Iron 3.4mg

¼ cup fat-free barbecue sauce
3 tablespoons low-sodium soy sauce
½ teaspoon dried crushed red pepper
Cooking spray
1 (¾-pound) pork tenderloin, cut into ¼-inch-thick slices
1¼ cups fresh baby carrots
1 (6-ounce) package frozen snow pea pods
3 cups hot cooked long-grain rice (cooked without salt or fat)

1. Combine first 3 ingredients; stir well, and set aside.

2. Coat a large nonstick skillet with cooking spray; place over medium heat until hot. Add pork, and cook 4 minutes or until browned, stirring occasionally.

3. Add sauce mixture and carrots to skillet; cover, reduce heat to medium-low, and simmer 7 minutes. Add snow peas; cook, uncovered, 4 minutes or until vegetables are crisp-tender. Serve over rice. Yield: 4 servings.

FOR A QUICK MEAL: Serve with Asian Coleslaw (page 183) and orange sherbet.

Sweet-and-Savory Pork Tenderloin

2   (½-pound) pork tenderloins
2   teaspoons ground sage
1   tablespoon salt-free lemon-herb seasoning
¼   cup apricot spreadable fruit
2   tablespoons Dijon mustard
Cooking spray

1. Slice pork lengthwise down center, cutting to, but not through bottom. Press with hands to flatten pork. Sprinkle sage and lemon-pepper seasoning over pork. Combine apricot spread and mustard. Spread half of apricot mixture over pork.

2. Coat grill rack with cooking spray, and place on grill over medium-hot coals (350° to 400°). Place tenderloins on rack; grill, covered, 7 minutes. Turn pork, and baste with remaining apricot mixture. Cover and grill 7 additional minutes or until a meat thermometer inserted into thickest part of tenderloin registers 160°. Yield: 4 servings.

FOR A QUICK MEAL: Serve with hash brown potatoes and green beans. If you don't want to butterfly the tenderloin, you can grill it, uncut, 10 minutes on each side or until done.

POINTS
4

EXCHANGES
3 Lean Meat
1 Fruit

PER SERVING
Calories 204
Carbohydrate 11.8g
Fat 5.1g (saturated 1.5g)
Fiber 0.5g
Protein 26.0g
Cholesterol 83mg
Sodium 284mg
Calcium 21mg
Iron 1.9mg

Ham Steak with Pineapple Salsa

POINTS

3

EXCHANGES

2 Very Lean Meat

1½ Fruit

PER SERVING

Calories 165

Carbohydrate 23.3g

Fat 3.4g (saturated 0.0g)

Fiber 0.5g

Protein 12.1g

Cholesterol 31mg

Sodium 563mg

Calcium 29mg

Iron 0.7mg

1   (15¼-ounce) can pineapple tidbits in juice, undrained

⅓   cup chopped green onions

2   tablespoons brown sugar

1   tablespoon cider vinegar

2   teaspoons low-sodium soy sauce

2   cloves garlic, minced

Cooking spray

¾   pound reduced-fat, lower-salt ham steak

1. Drain pineapple, reserving juice. Combine pineapple, 2 tablespoons pineapple juice, green onions, and next 4 ingredients in a bowl; stir well.

2. Coat grill rack with cooking spray; place on grill over medium-hot coals (350° to 400°). Place ham steak on rack, and grill, uncovered, about 4 minutes on each side, basting often with remaining pineapple juice. Serve ham steak with pineapple salsa. Yield: 4 servings.

 FOR A QUICK MEAL: Serve with Quick-Roasted Sweet Potatoes (page 185) and steamed broccoli.

poultry

Chicken Ravioli Primavera *(photo, page 120)*

POINTS

6

EXCHANGES

1 Medium-Fat Meat

2 Starch

2 Vegetable

PER SERVING

Calories 277

Carbohydrate 43.6g

Fat 4.8g (saturated 1.4g)

Fiber 2.2g

Protein 15.2g

Cholesterol 16mg

Sodium 827mg

Calcium 97mg

Iron 1.9mg

1	teaspoon olive oil
1½	teaspoons minced garlic
1	(28-ounce) can crushed tomatoes, undrained
2	teaspoons chopped fresh parsley
1	teaspoon dried oregano
½	teaspoon dried basil
¼	teaspoon sugar
2	cups sliced zucchini (about 1 large)
1	(25-ounce) package frozen chicken ravioli
2	tablespoons grated Parmesan or Romano cheese

Fresh basil sprigs (optional)

1. Heat oil in a large nonstick skillet over medium-high heat. Add garlic, and sauté 1 minute. Add tomatoes and next 4 ingredients. Bring to a boil. Reduce heat, and simmer, uncovered, 10 minutes, stirring occasionally. Add zucchini; cook 5 additional minutes or until tender.

2. While zucchini cooks, cook ravioli according to package directions. Drain well. Place on a large serving platter. Top with tomato mixture, and sprinkle with cheese. Garnish with basil sprigs, if desired. Yield: 6 servings.

 FOR A QUICK MEAL: Serve with a Caesar salad and warm dinner rolls.

Savory Chicken and Mushrooms

Cooking spray
2   (8-ounce) packages sliced fresh mushrooms
2   cups frozen diced cooked chicken breast
1   (10-ounce) container refrigerated light Alfredo sauce (s
      Contadina)
¾   teaspoon dried thyme
¼   teaspoon salt
¼   teaspoon pepper
2   tablespoons dry sherry
4   slices whole wheat bread, toasted

1. Coat a large nonstick skillet with cooking spray; place over medium-high heat until hot. Add mushrooms, and cook 5 minutes or until tender. Add chicken and next 4 ingredients; cook until thoroughly heated, stirring occasionally. Add sherry, stirring well.

2. Cut toast slices in half diagonally, and place on four individual serving plates. Spoon chicken mixture evenly over toast. Yield: 4 servings.

Ca
Carb
Fat 9.9
Fiber 2.6g
Protein 25.0
Cholesterol 64
Sodium 768mg
Calcium 149mg
Iron 3.0mg

FOR A QUICK MEAL: Serve with Maple-Glazed Carrots (page 184) and fresh spinach salad.

Creamed Chicken over Biscuits

POINTS

5

EXCHANGES

2 Very Lean Meat

1½ Starch

1 Vegetable

1 Fat

PER SERVING

Calories 254

Carbohydrate 28.1g

Fat 8.0g (saturated 2.2g)

Fiber 2.2g

Protein 17.6g

Cholesterol 38mg

Sodium 718mg

Calcium 0mg

Iron 1.5mg

1   (6-ounce) can flaky buttermilk biscuits (such as Hungry Jack)
Cooking spray
1   (9-ounce) package frozen diced cooked chicken breast
1   teaspoon minced garlic
1   (10-ounce) package frozen mixed vegetables, thawed and
        drained
1   (10¾-ounce) can cream of roasted chicken with savory herbs
        soup, undiluted (such as Campbell's Healthy Request)
¼   cup dry white wine
¼   cup water
¼   teaspoon pepper

1. Bake biscuits according to package directions; set aside, and keep warm.

2. While biscuits bake, coat a large nonstick skillet with cooking spray; place over medium-high heat until hot. Add chicken and garlic; cook 5 minutes, stirring occasionally. Stir in vegetables and remaining 4 ingredients; cook over medium heat 5 minutes or until vegetables are tender and thoroughly heated, stirring often.

3. Split each biscuit in half, and place on individual serving plates; spoon chicken mixture evenly over biscuits. Yield: 5 servings.

 FOR A QUICK MEAL: Serve with sliced tomatoes and Melon Boat with Frozen Yogurt (page 186).

Skillet Chicken Divan

1   family-size bag quick-cooking boil-in-bag rice
Cooking spray
1   (9-ounce) package frozen diced cooked chicken breast
½   (16-ounce) package fresh broccoli flowerets
2   tablespoons water
1   (10¾-ounce) can reduced-fat, reduced-sodium cream of
      chicken and broccoli soup, undiluted (such as Campbell's
      Healthy Request)
1   cup fat-free milk
½   cup (2 ounces) shredded reduced-fat sharp Cheddar cheese
½   teaspoon curry powder
¼   teaspoon salt
¼   teaspoon pepper

1. Cook rice according to package directions, omitting salt
and fat.

2. While rice cooks, coat a large nonstick skillet with cooking
spray; place over medium-high heat until hot. Add chicken and
broccoli; cook 6 minutes or until chicken is thawed and broccoli is
crisp-tender, adding 2 tablespoons water, if necessary, to prevent
sticking.

3. Combine soup and remaining 5 ingredients, stirring well. Add
to broccoli mixture. Cook, uncovered, over medium-low heat 10
minutes, stirring occasionally. Serve chicken mixture over rice.
Yield: 4 servings.

POINTS

8

EXCHANGES

3 Lean Meat

2½ Starch

2 Vegetable

PER SERVING

Calories 409

Carbohydrate 54.1g

Fat 7.6g (saturated 3.0g)

Fiber 2.2g

Protein 29.1g

Cholesterol 55mg

Sodium 703mg

Calcium 266mg

Iron 2.5mg

FOR A QUICK MEAL: Serve a simple fruit salad to round
out the meal.

Spinach Pesto Couscous

POINTS

6

EXCHANGES

2 Lean Meat

2 Starch

1 Vegetable

PER SERVING

Calories 301

Carbohydrate 34.5g

Fat 8.8g (saturated 1.1g)

Fiber 4.1g

Protein 23.1g

Cholesterol 37mg

Sodium 513mg

Calcium 86mg

Iron 2.1mg

1   teaspoon olive oil

¼   cup chopped walnuts

2   cups frozen diced cooked chicken breast, thawed

1⅓ cups water

1   (10-ounce) package frozen chopped spinach, thawed and
       well drained

1   (5.8-ounce) package roasted garlic and olive oil couscous

¼   cup thinly sliced fresh basil

1. Heat oil in a saucepan over medium-high heat; add walnuts, and cook 2 minutes or until toasted, stirring often. Remove walnuts from pan, and set aside.

2. Add chicken, water, spinach, contents of seasoning packet from couscous package, and basil to saucepan; cover, reduce heat, and simmer 2 minutes. Remove from heat, and stir in couscous. Cover and let stand 5 minutes. Stir in walnuts. Yield: 4 servings.

 FOR A QUICK MEAL: Serve with Parmesan Broiled Tomatoes (page 185) and warm focaccia.

Salsa Chicken on Polenta

1   (16-ounce) roll refrigerated Mexicana pepper-flavored polenta

Cooking spray

½   cup canned no-salt-added chicken broth

¾   cup mild chunky salsa

1   (15-ounce) can no-salt-added black beans, drained

1   (8¾-ounce) can no-salt-added whole-kernel corn, drained

1   (9-ounce) package frozen cooked chicken breast strips,
      thawed

½   teaspoon ground cumin

2   tablespoons chopped fresh cilantro (optional)

1. Cut polenta crosswise into ½-inch-thick slices; place on a baking sheet coated with cooking spray. Bake at 500° for 15 minutes or until thoroughly heated and golden around edges. Transfer polenta to individual serving plates, and keep warm.

2. While polenta bakes, combine broth and next 5 ingredients in a large skillet; cover and bring to a boil. Reduce heat to medium-low; simmer, uncovered, 10 minutes, stirring occasionally. Stir in cilantro, if desired. Spoon chicken mixture over polenta, and serve immediately. Yield: 4 servings.

 FOR A QUICK MEAL: Serve with Minted Strawberry-Pineapple Salad (page 182).

POINTS

4

EXCHANGES

3 Very Lean Meat

2 Starch

1 Vegetable

PER SERVING

Calories 291

Carbohydrate 43.1g

Fat 1.4g (saturated 0.8g)

Fiber 8.9g

Protein 25.3g

Cholesterol 34mg

Sodium 593mg

Calcium 76mg

Iron 3.2mg

RECIPE TIME: 9 minutes

Dijon Chicken Fettuccine

POINTS

3

EXCHANGES
2 Very Lean Meat
1 Starch
1 Vegetable

PER SERVING
Calories 162
Carbohydrate 22.9g
Fat 2.4g (saturated 0.6g)
Fiber 1.1g
Protein 12.5g
Cholesterol 54mg
Sodium 296mg
Calcium 25mg
Iron 0.6mg

1 (9-ounce) package refrigerated fettuccine
½ (16-ounce) package fresh broccoli flowerets (4 cups)
⅓ cup commercial fat-free honey Dijon dressing (such as Hellman's)
¼ cup red wine vinegar
1 tablespoon Dijon mustard
1 teaspoon olive oil
1 teaspoon bottled minced garlic
1 (10.11-ounce) package cooked chicken breast (such as Tyson's roasted chicken), skinned and shredded
¼ teaspoon freshly ground pepper

1. Cut pasta in half before cooking. Cook pasta according to package directions, omitting salt and fat. Add broccoli to pasta during last 3 minutes of cooking time. Drain well; place in a large bowl.

2. While pasta cooks, combine dressing and next 4 ingredients; stir well. Pour dressing mixture over pasta mixture. Add chicken, and toss gently. Sprinkle with pepper. Yield: 8 (1-cup) servings.

 FOR A QUICK MEAL: Serve with a romaine lettuce salad and Strawberry-Amaretto Smoothie (page 187).

Curry-Orange Chicken

2 cups instant rice, uncooked

¾ pound chicken breast tenders

2 tablespoons all-purpose flour

Cooking spray

1 teaspoon vegetable oil

2 medium-size green peppers, cut into strips

1 tablespoon minced garlic

½ cup canned no-salt-added chicken broth

⅓ cup low-sugar orange marmalade

1 teaspoon curry powder

POINTS

6

EXCHANGES

3 Very Lean Meat

2 Starch

1 Vegetable

½ Fruit

PER SERVING

Calories 323

Carbohydrate 47.1g

Fat 3.1g (saturated 0.6g)

Fiber 1.7g

Protein 24.6g

Cholesterol 49mg

Sodium 81mg

Calcium 37mg

Iron 3.6mg

1. Cook rice according to package directions, omitting salt and fat.

2. While rice cooks, combine chicken and flour in a zip-top plastic bag. Seal bag, and shake gently to coat chicken.

3. Coat a nonstick skillet with cooking spray; add oil. Place over medium-high heat until hot. Add pepper strips and garlic; cook, stirring constantly, 1 minute. Add chicken, and cook stirring constantly, 6 minutes or until chicken is lightly browned. Add broth, marmalade, and curry powder; cook 5 minutes or until chicken is done, stirring often. Serve over rice. Yield: 4 servings.

 FOR A QUICK MEAL: Serve with steamed broccoli sprinkled with toasted sesame seeds.

RECICE TIME: 20 minutes

Caribbean Chicken with Curry Sauce *(photo, page 118)*

POINTS
6

EXCHANGES
2 Very Lean Meat
2 Starch
1 Fruit

PER SERVING
Calories 294
Carbohydrate 49.1g
Fat 2.5g (saturated 0.4g)
Fiber 0.9g
Protein 19.2g
Cholesterol 44mg
Sodium 471mg
Calcium 28mg
Iron 1.5mg

2 regular-size bags quick-cooking boil-in-bag rice
Cooking spray
1 teaspoon margarine
½ cup finely chopped onion
2 cloves garlic, minced
1 pound chicken breast tenders
½ cup honey
¼ cup currants or raisins
¼ cup Dijon mustard
3 tablespoons mango chutney
1 teaspoon curry powder
¼ teaspoon salt

1. Cook rice according to package directions, omitting salt and fat.

2. Coat a large skillet with cooking spray; add margarine. Place over medium heat until hot. Add onion and garlic; cook, stirring constantly, 2 minutes. Add chicken, and cook, stirring constantly, 5 minutes or until chicken is browned. Add honey and remaining 5 ingredients, stirring well. Cover and simmer 10 minutes. Serve over rice. Yield: 6 servings.

 FOR A QUICK MEAL: Serve with steamed fresh spinach and Sliced Melon with Raspberry Sauce (page 182).

Chicken and Sugar Snap Sauté

1 (10-ounce) container refrigerated light Alfredo sauce (such as
    Contadina)
2 tablespoons fat-free milk or dry white wine
1 teaspoon olive oil
4 (4-ounce) skinned, boned chicken breast halves, cut into
    bite-size pieces
2 cups fresh Sugar Snap peas

1. Combine Alfredo sauce and milk, stirring well; set aside.

2. Heat oil in a large nonstick skillet over medium-high heat; add
chicken, and cook 7 minutes or until done, stirring occasionally.
Add peas, and cook 2 minutes. Add sauce mixture; bring to a boil,
stirring constantly. Serve immediately. Yield: 4 servings.

FOR A QUICK MEAL: Serve with cooked penne, rigatoni,
noodles, or white rice. For dessert, offer Butterscotch
Syrup Cake (page 187).

POINTS

5

EXCHANGES

4 Lean Meat

2 Vegetable

PER SERVING

Calories 251

Carbohydrate 10.7g

Fat 8.2g (saturated 3.9g)

Fiber 2.0g

Protein 32.3g

Cholesterol 89mg

Sodium 449mg

Calcium 168mg

Iron 1.1mg

Glazed Chicken-Broccoli Stir-Fry

POINTS
_____
8

EXCHANGES
_____
3 Very Lean Meat
3 Starch
2 Vegetable

PER SERVING
_____
Calories 396
Carbohydrate 58.0g
Fat 3.1g (saturated 0.6g)
Fiber 2.0g
Protein 32.1g
Cholesterol 66mg
Sodium 388mg
Calcium 80mg
Iron 3.0mg

1   family-size bag quick-cooking boil-in-bag rice or 3 cups hot
      cooked rice
Cooking spray
1   teaspoon vegetable oil
1   pound skinned, boned chicken breasts, cut into 1-inch pieces
3   cups broccoli flowerets
4   green onions, sliced
¼   cup spicy honey barbecue sauce
¼   cup frozen orange juice concentrate, thawed
¼   teaspoon dried crushed red pepper
¼   teaspoon salt

1. Cook rice according to package directions, omitting salt and fat.

2. While rice cooks, coat a large nonstick skillet with cooking spray; add oil to skillet. Place over medium-high heat until hot. Add chicken; stir-fry 3 minutes. Add broccoli and green onions; stir-fry 4 minutes. Combine barbecue sauce and remaining 3 ingredients; add to broccoli mixture. Cook over medium heat 3 to 4 minutes. Serve warm over rice. Yield: 4 servings.

 FOR A QUICK MEAL: Serve with Asian Coleslaw (page 183) and fortune cookies.

Creole Chicken Pasta

3   tablespoons all-purpose flour

2   teaspoons no-salt-added Creole seasoning, divided

4   (4-ounce) skinned, boned chicken breast halves, cut into
      strips

Cooking spray

2   teaspoons hot pepper oil

1   medium onion, cut into vertical strips (about 1 cup)

1   medium-size green pepper, cut into julienne strips

1   teaspoon minced garlic

1   (9-ounce) package refrigerated fettuccine

1   cup fat-free half-and-half or fat-free evaporated milk

POINTS

5

EXCHANGES

3 Very Lean Meat

1½ Starch

1 Vegetable

PER SERVING

Calories 269

Carbohydrate 32.2g

Fat 3.7g (saturated 0.5g)

Fiber 2.0g

Protein 23.4g

Cholesterol 44mg

Sodium 172mg

Calcium 42mg

Iron 1.7mg

1. Combine flour and 1½ teaspoons Creole seasoning in a large heavy-duty, zip-top plastic bag; add chicken, and shake to coat.

2. Coat a large nonstick skillet with cooking spray; add oil. Place over medium-high heat until hot. Add chicken, onion, pepper, and garlic; cook 8 to 10 minutes or until chicken is done and vegetables are tender, stirring occasionally.

3. While chicken mixture cooks, cook fettuccine according to package directions, omitting salt and fat; drain well.

4. Combine remaining ½ teaspoon Creole seasoning and half-and-half; add to chicken mixture in skillet, scraping bottom of skillet to deglaze. Cook 1 minute or until sauce is slightly thickened. Toss with cooked fettuccine; serve immediately. Yield: 6 (1-cup) servings.

 FOR A QUICK MEAL: Serve with a spinach salad and crusty French bread.

RECIPE TIME: 20 minutes

Chicken and Vegetable Pizzas

POINTS

8

EXCHANGES

3 Lean Meat

2½ Starch

1 Vegetable

PER SERVING

Calories 412

Carbohydrate 48.0g

Fat 7.1g (saturated 2.9g)

Fiber 2.5g

Protein 36.9g

Cholesterol 78mg

Sodium 866mg

Calcium 211mg

Iron 2.9mg

1   teaspoon seasoned pepper

2   (4-ounce) skinned, boned chicken breast halves

Cooking spray

1   large tomato, thinly sliced

½   cup sliced purple onion

¼   cup chopped fresh basil

¼   cup chopped fresh parsley

½   cup grated Parmesan cheese

4   (8-inch) pita bread rounds

½   cup commercial fat-free Ranch-style dressing

1. Sprinkle pepper over chicken. Coat grill rack with cooking spray; place on grill over medium-hot coals (350° to 400°). Place chicken on rack; grill, covered, 5 minutes on each side or until done. Cut chicken diagonally across the grain into thin strips.

2. Layer tomato and next 4 ingredients over pita rounds. Place on grill rack; grill 2 to 3 minutes or until bottom of pita is lightly browned. Drizzle 2 tablespoons dressing over each pita. Yield: 4 servings.

FOR A QUICK MEAL: Serve with a mixed greens salad drizzled with fat-free Italian dressing. For dessert, enjoy Dreamy Orange Smoothie (page 187).

Cinnamon-Grilled Chicken Breast

1   (8-ounce) can pineapple slices in juice, undrained
1   teaspoon low-sodium soy sauce
½   teaspoon ground cinnamon
4   (4-ounce) skinned, boned chicken breast halves
Cooking spray
8   lettuce leaves
½   cup mango chutney (such as Major Grey)

POINTS

6

EXCHANGES

3 Very Lean Meat
2½ Fruit

PER SERVING

Calories 297
Carbohydrate 37.5g
Fat 3.2g (saturated 0.8g)
Fiber 0.6g
Protein 26.3g
Cholesterol 70mg
Sodium 438mg
Calcium 33mg
Iron 1.4mg

1. Drain pineapple, reserving juice. Cover pineapple, and store in refrigerator. Combine reserved juice, soy sauce, and cinnamon in a large heavy-duty, zip-top plastic bag. Add chicken, and seal bag; turn to coat chicken. Marinate in refrigerator 8 hours, turning bag occasionally.

2. Coat grill rack with cooking spray; place on grill over medium-hot coals (350° to 400°). Remove chicken from marinade, discarding marinade. Place chicken on rack; grill, covered, 5 minutes on each side or until chicken is done, placing pineapple on grill during last 3 minutes of cooking.

3. Place lettuce leaves on four individual serving plates. Top evenly with chicken and pineapple. Spoon 2 tablespoons chutney over each serving. Yield: 4 servings.

 FOR A QUICK MEAL: Serve with couscous and steamed Brussels sprouts.

Grilled Chicken and Vegetables over Couscous

POINTS

7

EXCHANGES

3 Very Lean Meat

2½ Starch

2 Vegetable

PER SERVING

Calories 351

Carbohydrate 41.7g

Fat 4.5g (saturated 1.0g)

Fiber 3.3g

Protein 32.7g

Cholesterol 70mg

Sodium 613mg

Calcium 39mg

Iron 1.7mg

2	small zucchini
2	small yellow squash
1	small onion, sliced
4	(4-ounce) skinned, boned chicken breast halves
¼	cup plus 2 tablespoons commercial fat-free roasted garlic Italian dressing, divided

Cooking spray

1	(5.8-ounce) package roasted garlic and olive oil couscous

1. Cut zucchini and yellow squash in half lengthwise. Place zucchini, squash, onion, and chicken in a large heavy-duty, zip-top plastic bag; add ¼ cup dressing. Seal bag, and shake until vegetables and chicken are coated well.

2. Coat grill rack with cooking spray; place on grill over medium-hot coals (350° to 400°). Place chicken and vegetables on rack; grill, covered, 12 minutes or until chicken is done, turning once and basting occasionally with remaining 2 tablespoons dressing.

3. While chicken and vegetables cook, prepare couscous according to package directions, omitting fat. Spoon couscous onto a large serving platter. Top with grilled chicken and vegetables. Yield: 4 servings.

FOR A QUICK MEAL: Serve with sliced tomatoes and warm French bread. To heat the bread, wrap it in aluminum foil and place on grill with chicken.

Tropical Grilled Chicken

¾   teaspoon Jamaican jerk seasoning
4   (4-ounce) skinned, boned chicken breast halves
1   cup canned reduced-fat coconut milk
½   cup orange juice
1   tablespoon minced fresh basil
¼   teaspoon salt
Cooking spray
2   teaspoons flour

POINTS

4

EXCHANGES

3 Lean Meat

PER SERVING

Calories 179
Carbohydrate 5.3g
Fat 5.4g (saturated 2.2g)
Fiber 0.1g
Protein 26.6g
Cholesterol 70mg
Sodium 184mg
Calcium 18mg
Iron 1.0mg

1. Rub jerk seasoning on chicken. Combine coconut milk and next 3 ingredients in a small bowl. Pour half of mixture into a large heavy-duty, zip-top plastic bag; add chicken. Seal bag, and marinate in refrigerator at least 8 hours. Cover and store remaining coconut milk mixture in refrigerator.

2. Remove chicken from marinade, discarding marinade. Coat grill rack with cooking spray; place on grill over medium-hot coals (350° to 400°). Place chicken on rack; grill, covered, 5 minutes on each side or until done.

3. While chicken grills, pour reserved coconut milk mixture into a small saucepan; add flour. Place over medium-high heat. Bring to a boil; reduce heat, and simmer, uncovered, 5 minutes or until slightly thickened. Serve sauce over chicken. Yield: 4 servings.

 FOR A QUICK MEAL: Serve with sweet potatoes, steamed broccoli, and kiwifruit wedges.

Jalapeño Chicken *(photo, facing page)*

POINTS

2

EXCHANGES

3 Very Lean Meat

PER SERVING

Calories 109

Carbohydrate 4.1g

Fat 1.2g (saturated 0.3g)

Fiber 0.0g

Protein 19.2g

Cholesterol 48mg

Sodium 140mg

Calcium 12mg

Iron 0.6mg

$\frac{1}{3}$ cup steak sauce (such as Heinz 57)

$\frac{1}{3}$ cup jalapeño pepper jelly, melted

2   tablespoons low-sodium Worcestershire sauce

1   teaspoon garlic powder

4   (4-ounce) skinned, boned chicken breast halves

Cooking spray

1. Combine first 4 ingredients in a large heavy-duty, zip-top plastic bag. Add chicken; seal bag, and shake until chicken is coated well. Marinate in refrigerator 8 hours or overnight, turning bag occasionally.

2. Remove chicken from marinade, discarding marinade. Coat grill rack with cooking spray, and place on grill over medium-hot coals (350° to 400°). Place chicken on rack; grill, covered, 5 minutes on each side or until done. Yield: 4 servings.

FOR A QUICK MEAL: Serve with grilled slices of zucchini, yellow squash, and purple onion. For additional flavor, brush vegetables with remaining marinade before placing them in a grill basket. Serve with cooked rice or warm bread.

Caribbean Chicken
with Curry Sauce
(recipe, page 108)

Gingered Turkey and Asparagus
(recipe, page 129)

Chicken Ravioli
Primavera
(recipe, page 100)

Hawaiian Chicken with Pineapple Salsa

4   (4-ounce) skinned, boned chicken breast halves
1   teaspoon ground coriander
½   teaspoon salt
Cooking spray
¼   cup pineapple preserves, divided
1   (15¼-ounce) can pineapple tidbits in juice, drained
¼   cup chopped fresh cilantro
1   tablespoon seasoned rice vinegar
2   teaspoons minced jalapeño pepper

POINTS

5

EXCHANGES

3 Very Lean Meat
2 Fruit

PER SERVING

Calories 232
Carbohydrate 27.7g
Fat 1.7g (saturated 0.4g)
Fiber 0.6g
Protein 26.8g
Cholesterol 66mg
Sodium 377mg
Calcium 36mg
Iron 1.5mg

1. Place chicken between two sheets of heavy-duty plastic wrap, and flatten to ¼-inch thickness, using a meat mallet or rolling pin. Sprinkle chicken with coriander and salt; coat with cooking spray.

2. Coat a large nonstick skillet with cooking spray; place over medium heat until hot. Add chicken, and cook 5 to 6 minutes on each side or until chicken is done. Add 2 tablespoons preserves to skillet, and cook until chicken is glazed, turning once.

3. Combine remaining 2 tablespoons preserves, pineapple, and remaining 3 ingredients in a bowl; stir well. Serve with chicken. Yield: 4 servings.

FOR A QUICK MEAL: Serve with steamed white rice and Minted Peas (page 185).

Orange-Balsamic Chicken *(photo, page 4)*

POINTS

4

EXCHANGES

4 Very Lean Meat

½ Starch

PER SERVING

Calories 191

Carbohydrate 8.6g

Fat 4.3g (saturated 0.9g)

Fiber 0.2g

Protein 27.3g

Cholesterol 66mg

Sodium 260mg

Calcium 30mg

Iron 1.2mg

4   (4-ounce) skinned, boned chicken breast halves
¼   teaspoon salt
¼   teaspoon pepper
¼   cup all-purpose flour
1   tablespoon margarine
⅔   cup canned no-salt-added chicken broth
1½ teaspoons cornstarch
½   cup low-sugar orange marmalade
1½ tablespoons balsamic vinegar
Orange slices (optional)

1. Place chicken between two sheets of heavy-duty plastic wrap; flatten to ½-inch thickness, using a meat mallet or rolling pin. Sprinkle with salt and pepper; dredge in flour.

2. Melt margarine in a large nonstick skillet over medium-high heat. Add chicken, and cook 8 to 10 minutes or until done, turning once. Remove chicken from skillet; keep warm.

3. Combine broth and cornstarch; stir in marmalade. Stir broth mixture into skillet, and cook, stirring constantly, until mixture is thickened. Stir in vinegar. Reduce heat to medium; add chicken, turning to coat. Cook 1 to 2 additional minutes or until thoroughly heated. Garnish with orange slices, if desired. Yield: 4 servings.

> FOR A QUICK MEAL: A wonderful rich glaze dresses up this chicken for company. Serve with couscous and steamed green beans.

Pasta Primavera

1⅓ cups water

⅔ cup low-fat milk

1 (4.8-ounce) package angel hair pasta with herbs

1½ cups frozen mixed vegetables (such as broccoli, cauliflower, and carrots)

½ pound lean oven-roasted turkey breast (such as Healthy Choice), diced

½ cup diced roma tomatoes

2 tablespoons chopped fresh basil or parsley

1. Combine water and milk in a saucepan. Bring to a boil; reduce heat; slowly stir in pasta and contents of herb packet. Separate pasta with a fork, if necessary. Boil, uncovered, 4 to 5 minutes or until pasta is tender, stirring often. Remove from heat; let stand 2 to 3 minutes to thicken.

2. While pasta cooks, place frozen vegetables in a 1-quart microwave-safe baking dish. Cover with a paper towel; microwave at HIGH 5 minutes or until crisp-tender. Add vegetables, turkey, tomatoes, and basil to pasta mixture; toss well. Yield: 4 (1-cup) servings.

 FOR A QUICK MEAL: Serve with Italian Antipasto Salad (page 183) and soft breadsticks.

POINTS

4

EXCHANGES

2 Very Lean Meat

1½ Starch

1 Vegetable

PER SERVING

Calories 225

Carbohydrate 33.0g

Fat 3.4g (saturated 0.6g)

Fiber 3.8g

Protein 18.2g

Cholesterol 22mg

Sodium 935mg

Calcium 77mg

Iron 0.7mg

Polenta with Italian Meat Sauce

POINTS

4

EXCHANGES

2 Lean Meat

1½ Starch

1 Vegetable

PER SERVING

Calories 225

Carbohydrate 28.8g

Fat 5.5g (saturated 1.6g)

Fiber 4.2g

Protein 14.3g

Cholesterol 47mg

Sodium 977mg

Calcium 41mg

Iron 2.1mg

½ pound turkey Italian sausage

1 cup sliced fresh mushrooms

2 cups tomato-basil pasta sauce (such as Classico)

1 (16-ounce) package refrigerated sun-dried tomato-flavored
     polenta (such as Melissa's)

Cooking spray

Chopped fresh basil (optional)

1. Remove casings from sausage. Cook sausage and mushrooms in a large nonstick skillet over medium-high heat until sausage is browned, stirring until it crumbles.

2. Add pasta sauce to skillet; simmer, uncovered, 5 minutes.

3. While sauce simmers, cut polenta crosswise into 12 slices. Coat each side evenly with cooking spray. Place on a rack of a broiler pan. Broil 5½ inches from heat 4 minutes on each side or until golden.

4. Transfer polenta to individual serving plates; top with sauce mixture. Sprinkle with basil, if desired. Serve immediately. Yield: 4 servings.

 FOR A QUICK MEAL: Serve with a spinach salad and Chocolate-Berry Angel Cake (page 187).

Southwestern-Style Spaghetti

4   ounces spaghetti, uncooked
8   ounces freshly ground raw turkey breast
½   cup frozen chopped onion
1½   teaspoons bottled minced garlic
1   teaspoon ground cumin
1   (14½-ounce) can salsa-style tomatoes, undrained
½   cup picante sauce
¼   cup chopped fresh cilantro
2   tablespoons shredded part-skim mozzarella cheese

1. Cook spaghetti according to package directions, omitting salt and fat. Drain well, and place on a small serving platter.

2. While spaghetti cooks, cook turkey and next 3 ingredients in a large saucepan over medium heat until browned, stirring until turkey crumbles. Add tomatoes and picante sauce to turkey; simmer, uncovered, 10 minutes or until slightly thickened. Spoon over spaghetti; sprinkle with cilantro and cheese. Yield: 3 servings.

FOR A QUICK MEAL: Serve with a romaine and endive salad drizzled with fat-free Ranch-style dressing, and pass around a basket of chewy breadsticks.

POINTS
6

EXCHANGES
3 Very Lean Meat
2 Starch
2 Vegetables

PER SERVING
Calories 305
Carbohydrate 43.6g
Fat 2.7g (saturated 1.0g)
Fiber 4.0g
Protein 27.1g
Cholesterol 48mg
Sodium 917mg
Calcium 73mg
Iron 4.6mg

Balsamic Turkey

POINTS

3

EXCHANGES

3 Lean Meat

PER SERVING

Calories 157

Carbohydrate 2.5g

Fat 3.6g (saturated 1.0g)

Fiber 0.7g

Protein 27.1g

Cholesterol 68mg

Sodium 268mg

Calcium 17mg

Iron 2.0mg

6   (2-ounce) turkey breast cutlets
¼   teaspoon salt
¼   teaspoon garlic powder
¼   teaspoon pepper
Cooking spray
1   teaspoon olive oil
1   large red pepper, sliced into rings
¼   cup balsamic vinegar

1. Rub turkey with salt, garlic powder, and ¼ teaspoon pepper. Coat a large nonstick skillet with cooking spray. Add oil, and place skillet over medium-high heat until hot. Add turkey, and cook 2 minutes on each side or until lightly browned. Transfer cutlets to a serving platter; keep warm.

2. Add red pepper to skillet, and cook, stirring constantly, 3 minutes or until crisp-tender. Transfer red pepper to serving platter. Add vinegar to skillet; cook 2 minutes or until slightly reduced. Spoon over cutlets. Yield: 3 servings.

 FOR A QUICK MEAL: Serve with Greek Rice (page 185) and Sugar Snap peas.

Turkey Sauté with Cranberry-Port Sauce

1½ pounds turkey breast slices
1 teaspoon coarsely ground pepper
½ teaspoon salt
Cooking spray
1 (16-ounce) can whole-berry cranberry sauce
¼ cup port wine
3 tablespoons balsamic vinegar

1. Sprinkle turkey with pepper and salt. Coat a large nonstick skillet with cooking spray; place over medium-high heat until hot. Add half of turkey slices; cook 5 minutes or until browned on both sides, turning once. Remove from skillet, and keep warm. Repeat procedure with remaining turkey.

2. Add cranberry sauce, wine, and vinegar to skillet; bring to a boil. Return turkey to skillet; reduce heat, and simmer, uncovered, 3 minutes, basting turkey with sauce. Yield: 6 servings.

FOR A QUICK MEAL: This meal has the flavors of holiday favorites. Serve the turkey with mashed sweet potatoes and steamed broccoli.

POINTS
5

EXCHANGES
4 Very Lean Meat
2 Fruit

PER SERVING
Calories 253
Carbohydrate 29.8g
Fat 2.0g (saturated 0.6g)
Fiber 0.3g
Protein 26.9g
Cholesterol 68mg
Sodium 290mg
Calcium 19mg
Iron 1.7mg

Spicy Turkey Skillet

POINTS

4

EXCHANGES

4 Very Lean Meat

1½ Starch

1 Vegetable

PER SERVING

Calories 288

Carbohydrate 28.7g

Fat 2.6g (saturated 0.6g)

Fiber 8.7g

Protein 35.2g

Cholesterol 68mg

Sodium 327mg

Calcium 136mg

Iron 3.1mg

1   (15-ounce) can no-salt-added black beans, drained
1   (10-ounce) can diced tomatoes and green chiles, undrained
1   (8¾-ounce) can no-salt-added whole-kernel corn, drained
2   tablespoons chopped fresh cilantro or parsley
1   teaspoon ground cumin
½   teaspoon hot sauce
Cooking spray
1   pound turkey breast tenderloin, cut into 1-inch pieces
¾   cup chopped onion
½   teaspoon bottled minced garlic or 1 clove garlic, minced

1. Combine first 6 ingredients in a bowl; set aside.

2. Coat a large nonstick skillet with cooking spray; place over medium-high heat until hot. Add turkey, onion, and garlic; cook, stirring constantly, until turkey is browned. Stir in bean mixture; bring to a boil. Reduce heat, and simmer, uncovered, 5 to 7 minutes or until turkey is done and most of liquid is evaporated, stirring occasionally. Yield: 4 servings.

FOR A QUICK MEAL: This is a superquick one-dish meal that's hearty and liked by kids. Serve with Apple Pie Sundae (page 186).

Gingered Turkey and Asparagus *(photo, page 119)*

1	pound turkey breast tenderloin
Cooking spray	
16	asparagus spears
¾	cup canned fat-free reduced-sodium chicken broth
¼	cup orange juice
¾	teaspoon ground ginger
¼	teaspoon pepper
1	tablespoon water
2	teaspoons cornstarch

POINTS
3

EXCHANGES
3 Very Lean Meat
1 Vegetable

PER SERVING
Calories 162
Carbohydrate 6.0g
Fat 2.0g (saturated 0.6g)
Fiber 1.3g
Protein 28.7g
Cholesterol 68mg
Sodium 163mg
Calcium 28mg
Iron 1.9mg

1. Place turkey between two sheets of heavy-duty plastic wrap; flatten to ½-inch thickness, using a meat mallet or rolling pin. Coat a large nonstick skillet with cooking spray, and place over medium-high heat until hot. Add turkey, and cook 5 to 6 minutes on each side or until lightly browned. Add asparagus and next 4 ingredients. Bring to a boil; cover, reduce heat, and simmer 6 to 8 minutes or until turkey is done.

2. Combine water and cornstarch, stirring well. Add cornstarch mixture to turkey mixture in skillet; cook, stirring constantly, 1 minute or until sauce is thickened. Remove turkey and asparagus from skillet, and place on a serving platter. Spoon sauce over turkey and asparagus. Yield: 4 servings.

 FOR A QUICK MEAL: Serve with fresh orange slices and a bowl of noodles.

Penne with Beans and Sausage

POINTS

3

EXCHANGES

2 Very Lean Meat

1½ Starch

1 Vegetable

PER SERVING

Calories 223

Carbohydrate 38.1g

Fat 1.6g (saturated 0.0g)

Fiber 5.5g

Protein 13.8g

Cholesterol 13mg

Sodium 262mg

Calcium 36mg

Iron 1.9mg

8   ounces sun-dried tomato-flavored or plain penne pasta,
      uncooked (such as Mendocino)

6   ounces fat-free smoked turkey sausage (such as Butterball)

Cooking spray

½   cup canned fat-free reduced-sodium chicken broth

1   cup canned cannellini beans, rinsed and drained

2   cups loosely packed baby spinach leaves or torn spinach leaves

3   tablespoons red wine vinegar

1   large tomato, chopped

1. Cook pasta according to package directions, omitting salt and fat. Drain well, and return to saucepan.

2. While pasta cooks, cut sausage in half lengthwise; cut each half into thin slices. Coat a large nonstick skillet with cooking spray; add sausage, and cook 4 minutes, stirring occasionally. Add broth and beans; cook until thoroughly heated.

3. Add sausage mixture, spinach, vinegar, and tomato to pasta; toss well. Yield: 6 (1½-cup) servings.

 FOR A QUICK MEAL: Serve with crusty French bread and Peachy Parfaits (page 187).

main-dish salads

Bean and Pasta Salad *(photo, page 138)*

POINTS

5

EXCHANGES
1 Very Lean Meat
3 Starch
1 Vegetable

PER SERVING
Calories 276
Carbohydrate 51.6g
Fat 2.3g (saturated 0.7g)
Fiber 3.5g
Protein 12.3g
Cholesterol 2mg
Sodium 659mg
Calcium 74mg
Iron 1.9mg

8	ounces farfalle (bow tie pasta), uncooked
1	(15-ounce) can no-salt-added black beans, rinsed and drained
1	pint cherry tomatoes, halved
1	medium-size green bell pepper, chopped
1	large lime, cut in half
2	tablespoons chopped fresh cilantro
2	cloves garlic, minced
1	cup commercial fat-free Italian dressing
3	tablespoons freshly grated Parmesan cheese

1. Cook pasta according to package directions, omitting salt and fat.

2. While pasta cooks, place beans, tomatoes, and pepper in a large bowl. Squeeze lime juice over bean mixture; discard lime rind. Add cilantro and garlic to bean mixture.

3. Drain pasta; add to bean mixture. Pour dressing over salad, tossing gently to coat; sprinkle with cheese. Cover and chill at least 8 hours. Yield: 6 (1½-cup) servings.

 FOR A QUICK MEAL: Serve with Lemon-Pepper Corn on the Cob (page 184) and toasted pita chips.

Lemony Bean and Tuna Salad

¼   cup chopped green onions
1   teaspoon grated lemon rind
1   tablespoon dried basil
2   tablespoons fresh lemon juice
1   tablespoon white wine vinegar
1   teaspoon olive oil
1   cup cherry tomatoes, quartered
1   (15-ounce) can cannellini beans, rinsed and drained
1   (6-ounce) can chunk white tuna in water, drained and flaked

1. Combine first 6 ingredients in a large bowl, stirring well. Add tomatoes, beans, and tuna; toss gently. Cover and chill at least 1 hour. Yield: 3 (1-cup) servings.

 FOR A QUICK MEAL: Serve with soft breadsticks and a fruit sorbet.

POINTS

3

EXCHANGES

2 Very Lean Meat
½ Starch
1 Vegetable

PER SERVING

Calories 144
Carbohydrate 15.5g
Fat 2.4g (saturated 0.3g)
Fiber 0.8g
Protein 14.7g
Cholesterol 12mg
Sodium 26mg
Calcium 49mg
Iron 2.6mg

Salad Niçoise *(photo, page 1)*

POINTS

5

EXCHANGES

4 Very Lean Meat

1½ Starch

1 Vegetable

PER SERVING

Calories 279

Carbohydrate 26.5g

Fat 6.2g (saturated 1.5g)

Fiber 3.8g

Protein 30.5g

Cholesterol 43mg

Sodium 173mg

Calcium 37mg

Iron 3.4mg

3	small round red potatoes, sliced
¼	pound fresh green beans, trimmed
1	(8-ounce) tuna steak (¾ inch thick)
⅓	cup white wine vinegar
1½	tablespoons lemon juice
1½	teaspoons Dijon mustard
2	cups torn Bibb lettuce or leaf lettuce
1	medium tomato, cut into eight wedges
¼	teaspoon freshly ground pepper

1. Arrange potato and green beans on one side of a steamer basket over boiling water in a Dutch oven. Place tuna on opposite side of basket. Cover and steam 8 to 10 minutes or until fish flakes easily when tested with a fork. Set tuna aside to cool. Plunge potato and beans into ice water to cool.

2. While tuna and vegetables steam, combine vinegar, lemon juice, and mustard in a jar; cover tightly, and shake vigorously.

3. Place lettuce on a serving platter. Drain potato and beans; arrange over lettuce. Flake tuna, and place on salad; add tomato wedges. Drizzle with vinegar mixture. Sprinkle with freshly ground pepper. Yield: 2 servings.

FOR A QUICK MEAL: Serve with French bread and Strawberry Trifle (page 187).

Shrimp and Couscous Salad

1¼ cups water

1 (5.9-ounce) package Parmesan-flavored couscous

½ pound cooked, peeled large fresh shrimp

1 (14-ounce) can quartered artichoke hearts, drained

1 (7.25-ounce) jar roasted red peppers, drained and chopped

1 (2¼-ounce) can sliced ripe olives, drained

½ cup sliced green onions

1 teaspoon dried basil

1 teaspoon dried oregano

¼ teaspoon pepper

1 clove garlic, minced

¼ cup fat-free red wine vinaigrette (such as Girard's)

½ cup crumbled feta cheese

POINTS

5

EXCHANGES

1½ Lean Meat

2 Starch

2 Vegetable

PER SERVING

Calories 283

Carbohydrate 41.3g

Fat 5.1g (saturated 2.4g)

Fiber 3.3g

Protein 18.3g

Cholesterol 102mg

Sodium 1219mg

Calcium 137mg

Iron 3.5mg

1. Bring water to a boil in a medium saucepan. Remove from heat; stir in couscous and spice packet from couscous. Cover and let stand 5 minutes. Fluff with a fork.

2. Combine couscous, shrimp, and next 8 ingredients in a bowl. Drizzle vinaigrette over salad; toss well. Sprinkle with feta cheese. Yield: 5 (1-cup) servings.

 FOR A QUICK MEAL: Serve with warm whole grain bread and Dreamy Orange Smoothie (page 187).

Asian Shrimp and Chick-Pea Salad

POINTS

5

EXCHANGES

2 Lean Meat

1½ Starch

2 Vegetable

PER SERVING

Calories 274

Carbohydrate 33.8g

Fat 5.5g (saturated 0.9g)

Fiber 4.0g

Protein 23.0g

Cholesterol 115mg

Sodium 295mg

Calcium 90mg

Iron 4.4mg

2 cups cooked instant brown rice

1½ cups fresh bean sprouts

⅓ cup diagonally sliced green onions

1 pound cooked, peeled medium-size fresh shrimp

1 (15½-ounce) can chick-peas (garbanzo beans), rinsed and
    drained

1 (6-ounce) package snow peas, thawed

¼ cup rice vinegar

1 tablespoon low-sodium soy sauce

1 tablespoon dark sesame oil

2 teaspoons water

1½ teaspoons peeled, grated gingerroot

½ teaspoon brown sugar

¼ teaspoon pepper

1. Combine first 6 ingredients in a large bowl; toss well.

2. Combine vinegar and remaining 6 ingredients; stir well with
a wire whisk. Pour over rice mixture; toss well. Cover and chill
until ready to serve. Yield: 6 (1⅓-cup) servings.

 FOR A QUICK MEAL: Serve with sesame crackers and
Citrus with Granola Crunch (page 186).

New Wave Chef's Salad
with Garlic Croutons
(recipe, page 143)

Bean and Pasta Salad
(recipe, page 132)

Grilled Jerk
Chicken Salad
(recipe, page 149)

Steak Caesar Salad for Two *(photo, facing page)*

1   tablespoon salt-free lemon-pepper seasoning
½   pound boneless beef sirloin steak (¾ inch thick)
Cooking spray
5   cups torn romaine lettuce
¼   cup commercial fat-free seasoned croutons
¼   cup commercial fat-free Caesar-style dressing
6   cherry tomatoes, halved

1. Rub lemon-pepper seasoning on both sides of steak; place steak on rack of a broiler pan coated with cooking spray. Broil 3 inches from heat 2 to 3 minutes on each side or to desired degree of doneness.

2. While steak broils, combine lettuce and remaining 3 ingredients in a large bowl; toss gently. Arrange on two individual salad plates.

3. Slice steak into thin strips, and arrange over lettuce. Yield: 2 servings.

FOR A QUICK MEAL: Serve with toasted French bread slices. Before toasting, lightly spray each slice with olive oil-flavored cooking spray and sprinkle with garlic powder.

POINTS

6

EXCHANGES

3 Lean Meat

½ Starch

2 Vegetable

PER SERVING

Calories 271

Carbohydrate 20.2g

Fat 7.1g (saturated 2.6g)

Fiber 2.0g

Protein 30.0g

Cholesterol 80mg

Sodium 535mg

Calcium 42mg

Iron 4.1mg

Sliced Beef with Lettuce, Cucumber, and Tomatoes

POINTS

3

EXCHANGES

2 Lean Meat

2 Vegetable

PER SERVING

Calories 160

Carbohydrate 10.7g

Fat 6.9g (saturated 2.8g)

Fiber 2.3g

Protein 13.6g

Cholesterol 30mg

Sodium 645mg

Calcium 22mg

Iron 1.9mg

¼   cup reduced-sodium soy sauce
¼   teaspoon ground ginger
¾   pound lean flank steak
Cooking spray
1   (10-ounce) package torn Italian salad mix
2   cups thinly sliced English cucumber or salad cucumber
2   medium tomatoes, quartered
½   large purple onion, thinly sliced
2   tablespoons reduced-sodium soy sauce
2   tablespoons rice vinegar
½   teaspoon dried crushed red pepper

1. Combine ¼ cup soy sauce and ginger, stirring well. Place steak on rack of a broiler pan coated with cooking spray; brush both sides of steak with soy sauce mixture.

2. Broil steak 3 inches from heat 10 minutes or to desired degree of doneness, turning once and basting with remaining soy sauce mixture. Cut steak diagonally across the grain into thin slices.

3. Arrange salad greens on a large serving platter. Arrange steak, cucumber, tomato, and onion over greens. Combine 2 tablespoons soy sauce, vinegar, and pepper, stirring well; drizzle over salad. Yield: 6 servings.

FOR A QUICK MEAL: When served on a platter, this entrée is especially attractive on a buffet. Serve with warm sourdough rolls. For dessert, offer Melon Boat with Frozen Yogurt (page 186).

New Wave Chef's Salad with Garlic Croutons *(photo, page 137)*

4   ounces French bread, cut into 12 slices
Garlic-flavored cooking spray
2   tablespoons chopped walnuts
8   cups packed mixed baby salad greens
1   ripe pear, cored and diced (about 1¼ cup)
4   ounces reduced-sodium deli ham, cut into thin strips
¼   cup crumbled blue cheese
⅓   cup commercial fat-free raspberry vinaigrette

1. Spray both sides of bread slices with cooking spray. Arrange bread on a large baking sheet, and bake at 400° for 4 minutes. Turn bread; add walnuts, and bake 4 additional minutes or until croutons are golden.

2. While croutons bake, arrange salad greens on four individual salad plates. Arrange pear, ham, and cheese over greens. Drizzle vinaigrette evenly over salads, and sprinkle with walnuts. Serve with toasted croutons. Yield: 4 servings.

POINTS

4

EXCHANGES

1 Lean Meat
1 Starch
1 Vegetable
½ Fruit

PER SERVING

Calories 203
Carbohydrate 26.8g
Fat 6.4g (saturated 1.7g)
Fiber 2.7g
Protein 11.1g
Cholesterol 20mg
Sodium 638mg
Calcium 115mg
Iron 2.0mg

FOR A QUICK MEAL: Serve with slices of angel food cake topped with fresh strawberries.

Black Bean and Pork Salad

POINTS

4

EXCHANGES

3 Lean Meat

1 Starch

1 Fruit

PER SERVING

Calories 279

Carbohydrate 28.0g

Fat 6.4g (saturated 2.1g)

Fiber 8.3g

Protein 26.9g

Cholesterol 54mg

Sodium 74mg

Calcium 87mg

Iron 1.9mg

Cooking spray

¾ pound lean boneless pork loin, cut into thin strips

1 teaspoon minced garlic

½ cup orange juice

2 tablespoons red wine vinegar

¼ teaspoon ground red pepper

¼ teaspoon ground ginger

1 small head Bibb lettuce

1 (15-ounce) can no-salt-added black beans, drained

1 (26-ounce) jar orange sections, drained, or 4 large navel
    oranges, peeled and sectioned

1 green onion, sliced

1. Coat a large nonstick skillet with cooking spray; place over medium-high heat until hot. Add pork and garlic; cook 3 minutes or until pork is done, stirring often.

2. Combine orange juice and next 3 ingredients in a small bowl, beating with a wire whisk until blended.

3. Wash lettuce leaves; arrange on a serving platter. Arrange beans, pork, and orange sections over lettuce leaves. Drizzle with orange juice mixture, and sprinkle with green onions. Yield: 4 servings.

FOR A QUICK MEAL: Serve with wedges of cornbread. If you don't have orange juice on hand, use ½ cup of the juice from the jar of orange sections.

Warm Pork and Peanut Salad

1	(1-pound) extra-lean pork tenderloin (such as Smithfield)
3	tablespoons low-sodium soy sauce
2	tablespoons rice wine vinegar
1	tablespoon Thai chili paste
¼	teaspoon sugar
Cooking spray	
5	cups packaged coleslaw (in the produce section)
1	tablespoon roasted unsalted peanuts, coarsely chopped

POINTS

4

EXCHANGES

3 Lean Meat

2 Vegetable

PER SERVING

Calories 184

Carbohydrate 9.9g

Fat 9.2g (saturated 1.2g)

Fiber 2.7g

Protein 26.4g

Cholesterol 60mg

Sodium 558mg

Calcium 48mg

Iron 1.7mg

1. Cut pork crosswise into ¼-inch slices. Combine soy sauce and next 3 ingredients in a bowl. Add pork; toss to coat.

2. Coat a large nonstick skillet with cooking spray; place over medium-high heat until hot. Add pork, reserving remaining soy sauce mixture. Cook 5 minutes or until pork is done, stirring occasionally. Add reserved soy sauce mixture; bring to a boil. Reduce heat; simmer 30 seconds.

3. Place coleslaw in a bowl; spoon pork mixture over coleslaw, and toss well. Sprinkle with peanuts. Yield: 4 (1¼-cup) servings.

 FOR A QUICK MEAL: Serve with crusty rolls and mandarin orange sections.

Apricot-Cashew Chicken Salad

POINTS

3

EXCHANGES

2 Very Lean Meat

1 Vegetable

1 Fruit

PER SERVING

Calories 182

Carbohydrate 19.9g

Fat 3.2g (saturated 1.0g)

Fiber 2.4g

Protein 17.0g

Cholesterol 31mg

Sodium 336mg

Calcium 31mg

Iron 1.4mg

1	(16½-ounce) can apricot halves in extra-light syrup, sliced
1	tablespoon sugar
3	tablespoons lemon juice
1	teaspoon ground cumin
1	teaspoon low-sodium soy sauce
4	cups torn romaine lettuce (about half of a 10-ounce bag)
1	(10-ounce) can chicken chunks in water, drained
1	cup bean sprouts
¼	cup chopped green onions (about 2)
2	tablespoons chopped unsalted cashews

1. Drain apricots, reserving 2 tablespoons syrup. Set apricots aside.

2. Combine reserved syrup, sugar, and next 3 ingredients in a small bowl, stirring well.

3. Combine lettuce, apricots, and remaining 4 ingredients in a large bowl. Pour dressing over salad; toss well. Yield: 4 (2-cup) servings.

 FOR A QUICK MEAL: Serve with focaccia and Butterscotch Syrup Cake (page 187).

Bulgur Chicken Salad

2	cups water
1	cup bulgur, uncooked
2	cups frozen diced cooked chicken, thawed
1	cup chopped green onions (about 8)
2	tablespoons lemon juice
1	teaspoon olive oil
¼	teaspoon salt
1	(8-ounce) can pineapple tidbits in juice, undrained
1	sweet red pepper, finely chopped
½	cup chopped fresh parsley (optional)

Dash of hot sauce (optional)

1. Bring water to a boil in a medium saucepan. Stir in bulgur; cover and simmer 15 minutes or until water is absorbed. Remove from heat, and fluff with a fork.

2. While bulgar cooks, combine chicken and next 6 ingredients; if desired, add parsley and hot sauce. Add to cooked bulgur, stirring well. Yield: 4 servings.

 FOR A QUICK MEAL: Serve warm on a bed of lettuce leaves. Enjoy any leftovers as a chilled salad for lunch.

POINTS

4

EXCHANGES

2 Lean Meat

1 Starch

1 Vegetable

1 Fruit

PER SERVING

Calories 262

Carbohydrate 39.5g

Fat 4.2g (saturated 1.0g)

Fiber 8.0g

Protein 19.4g

Cholesterol 37mg

Sodium 262mg

Calcium 49mg

Iron 2.7mg

Chicken Salad with Brown Rice

POINTS

5

EXCHANGES

2 Lean Meat

2 Starch

1 Vegetable

PER SERVING

Calories 262

Carbohydrate 46.4g

Fat 4.6g (saturated 1.6g)

Fiber 4.1g

Protein 17.7g

Cholesterol 44mg

Sodium 889mg

Calcium 24mg

Iron 0.5mg

2	cups instant brown rice, uncooked
2	cups shredded roasted chicken breast (such as Tyson)
1	cup packaged shredded carrot
¾	cup fat-free balsamic vinaigrette
⅓	cup chopped green onions (about 3)
3	tablespoons raisins
1	large cucumber, chopped
2	medium-size sweet red peppers, halved (optional)

Lettuce leaves (optional)

1. Cook rice according to package directions, omitting salt and fat.

2. Combine cooked rice, chicken, and next 5 ingredients in a large bowl; toss to combine. Serve immediately, or chill overnight. If desired, serve in red pepper halves or on lettuce leaves. Yield: 4 (1½-cup) servings.

> FOR A QUICK MEAL: If your grocery store doesn't have packaged roasted chicken, you can pick up a roasted chicken at its deli or use leftover roasted chicken. Serve with Peachy Parfaits (page 187).

Grilled Jerk Chicken Salad *(photo, page 139)*

5   green onions, sliced and divided
3   tablespoons fresh lime juice
2   tablespoons habanero pepper sauce
1   tablespoon white vinegar
2½ tablespoons salt-free Jamaican jerk seasoning blend
4   (4-ounce) skinned, boned chicken breast halves
Cooking spray
8   cups mixed salad greens
2   ripe mangoes, peeled and cubed
¾   cup fat-free mango dressing

POINTS
5

EXCHANGES
3 Very Lean Meat
2 Vegetable
1 Fruit

PER SERVING
Calories 241
Carbohydrate 25.3g
Fat 3.5g (saturated 0.9g)
Fiber 2.6g
Protein 27.4g
Cholesterol 70mg
Sodium 164mg
Calcium 55mg
Iron 1.9mg

1. Combine 2 tablespoons green onions and next 4 ingredients in container of an electric blender; cover and process until smooth. Brush both sides of chicken breast halves with green onion mixture.

2. Coat grill rack with cooking spray; place over medium-hot coals (350° to 400°). Place chicken on rack, and grill, covered, 5 minutes on each side or until done. Cut chicken crosswise into ¼-inch-thick strips.

3. Place 2 cups salad greens on each individual serving plate; top evenly with mango and remaining green onions. Arrange chicken over salads; top each serving with 3 tablespoons dressing. Yield: 4 servings.

 FOR A QUICK MEAL: Serve with crisp sesame breadsticks and Strawberry-Amaretto Smoothie (page 187).

Thai Chicken Salad

POINTS

3

EXCHANGES

3 Very Lean Meat

1 Vegetable

PER SERVING

Calories 160

Carbohydrate 4.2g

Fat 2.9g (saturated 0.6g)

Fiber 1.6g

Protein 27.2g

Cholesterol 66mg

Sodium 325mg

Calcium 48mg

Iron 1.5mg

Cooking spray

4   (4-ounce) skinned, boned chicken breast halves, cut into 1-inch pieces

3   stalks celery, diagonally sliced into 1-inch pieces

2   small carrots, diagonally sliced

¼ cup canned fat-free, low-sodium chicken broth (such as Campbell's Healthy Request)

2   tablespoons low-sodium soy sauce

1   tablespoon rice wine vinegar

1   teaspoon dark sesame oil

4   cups mixed salad greens

1. Coat a large nonstick skillet with cooking spray; place over medium-high heat until hot. Add chicken; stir-fry 5 minutes or until done. Remove chicken from skillet; keep warm.

2. Add celery and carrot to skillet; stir-fry 1 minute or until crisp-tender. Keep warm.

3. Combine chicken broth and next 3 ingredients in a large bowl, stirring with a wire whisk. Add salad greens, chicken, and celery mixture; toss well. Serve immediately. Yield: 4 servings.

FOR A QUICK MEAL: Start your meal with egg drop soup. For four servings, bring 4 cups chicken broth to a boil. Add ¼ cup each chopped green onions and chopped parsley. Lightly beat 2 eggs with 2 tablespoons lemon juice. Gradually stir into hot broth. Cook over medium heat 5 minutes.

soups & sandwiches

Corn, Leek, and Potato Chowder

POINTS

5

EXCHANGES

2 Lean Meat

1½ Starch

1 Vegetable

PER SERVING

Calories 250

Carbohydrate 34.0g

Fat 6.2g (saturated 3.4g)

Fiber 3.3g

Protein 17.2g

Cholesterol 21mg

Sodium 603mg

Calcium 431mg

Iron 1.2mg

Cooking spray

1   cup sliced leek (about 2 small)

2   cups frozen hash brown potatoes with peppers and onions (such as O'Brien style), thawed

1   (10-ounce) package frozen whole-kernel corn, thawed

½   teaspoon salt

¼   teaspoon freshly ground pepper

2½ cups fat-free milk

1   cup (4 ounces) reduced-fat shredded Cheddar cheese

1. Coat a large saucepan with cooking spray; place over medium-high heat until hot. Add leek, and cook, stirring constantly, 2 minutes. Add hash brown potatoes and next 3 ingredients; cook 3 minutes, stirring occasionally.

2. Add milk to potato mixture; bring to a boil. Reduce heat; simmer, uncovered, 8 minutes, stirring often. Ladle chowder into bowls; top with cheese. Yield: 4 (1-cup) servings.

 FOR A QUICK MEAL: Serve with a romaine lettuce salad and whole wheat rolls.

RECIPE TIME: 20 minutes

Lemon-Tortellini Soup

Cooking spray
1   cup sliced fresh mushrooms
½   cup sliced green onions
1   clove garlic, minced
2   (14¼-ounce) cans no-salt-added chicken broth
¼   teaspoon salt
1   (10-ounce) package frozen broccoli flowerets, thawed
1   (9-ounce) package refrigerated cheese-filled tortellini
2   tablespoons lemon juice

1. Coat a Dutch oven with cooking spray; place over medium-high heat until hot. Add mushrooms, green onions, and garlic; cook 5 minutes or until vegetables are tender, stirring occasionally.

2. Add broth and salt to mushroom mixture; bring to a boil. Add broccoli; cover, reduce heat, and simmer 5 minutes. Add tortellini; cook 5 minutes or until tender. Stir in lemon juice. Yield: 6 (1-cup) servings.

 FOR A QUICK MEAL: Serve with Parmesan Broiled Tomatoes (page 185) and breadsticks.

POINTS

3

EXCHANGES

1½ Starch

1 Vegetable

½ Fat

PER SERVING

Calories 160

Carbohydrate 25.2g

Fat 2.3g

Fiber 2.8g

Protein 9.2g

Cholesterol 20mg

Sodium 267mg

Calcium 133mg

Iron 1.8mg

Spicy Tomato-Fish Chowder

POINTS

3

EXCHANGES

2 Very Lean Meat

½ Starch

1 Vegetable

PER SERVING

Calories 135

Carbohydrate 10.3g

Fat 1.0g (saturated 0.2g)

Fiber 0.1g

Protein 18.8g

Cholesterol 34mg

Sodium 237mg

Calcium 29mg

Iron 1.1mg

Cooking spray

1 (10-ounce) package frozen chopped onion, celery, and pepper seasoning blend

1½ cups frozen cubed hash brown potatoes

½ teaspoon garlic powder

1 cup water

½ cup dry white wine

1 (10-ounce) can diced tomatoes and green chiles, undrained

1½ pounds grouper, skinned and cut into 1-inch pieces

1. Coat a Dutch oven with cooking spray; place over medium-high heat until hot. Add frozen seasoning blend, potatoes, and garlic powder; cook, stirring constantly, 5 minutes. Stir in water, wine, and tomatoes and green chiles. Bring to a boil. Cover, reduce heat, and simmer 8 minutes.

2. Add fish to potato mixture; cover and simmer 4 minutes or until fish flakes easily when tested with a fork. Yield: 7 (1-cup) servings.

 FOR A QUICK MEAL: Serve with corn sticks and fat-free marinated coleslaw.

Shrimp Chowder

Cooking spray

1½ cups frozen chopped onion, celery, and pepper seasoning
  blend

3 (15-ounce) cans reduced-fat baked potato-style soup (such as
  Healthy Choice)

2 (7-ounce) cans tiny shrimp, rinsed and drained

2½ cups fat-free milk

¼ teaspoon pepper

1. Coat a large saucepan with cooking spray; place over medium
heat until hot. Add frozen seasoning blend, and cook 5 minutes,
stirring occasionally.

2. Add potato soup and remaining ingredients. Cook over medium-
high heat 5 to 7 minutes or until thoroughly heated, stirring occasionally. Yield: 9 (1-cup) servings.

 FOR A QUICK MEAL: Serve with Asparagus Salad with
Blue Cheese (page 183).

POINTS

3

EXCHANGES

1 Lean Meat

1 Vegetable

1 Skim Milk

PER SERVING

Calories 155

Carbohydrate 20.9g

Fat 2.1g (saturated 0.9g)

Fiber 2.7g

Protein 13.8g

Cholesterol 57mg

Sodium 406mg

Calcium 141mg

Iron 1.0mg

Beefy Minestrone Soup

POINTS

2

EXCHANGES

1 Very Lean Meat

1 Starch

1 Vegetable

PER SERVING

Calories 157

Carbohydrate 20.7g

Fat 1.8g (saturated 0.7g)

Fiber 4.4g

Protein 13.5g

Cholesterol 20mg

Sodium 303mg

Calcium 49mg

Iron 2.4mg

2   (14¼-ounce) cans fat-free no-salt-added beef broth (such as Health Valley)

1   (14½-ounce) can no-salt-added stewed tomatoes, undrained

⅔   cup ditalini pasta, uncooked

1   large zucchini

1   (15.5-ounce) can cannellini beans, rinsed and drained

2   teaspoons dried Italian seasoning

8   ounces deli rare roast beef, sliced ¼-inch thick and diced

1. Combine first 3 ingredients in a large saucepan; cover and bring to a boil over high heat.

2. While pasta mixture comes to a boil, cut zucchini in half lengthwise, and slice. Add zucchini, beans, and Italian seasoning to pasta; cover, reduce heat, and simmer 6 minutes. Add beef, and cook 4 additional minutes or until pasta is tender. Yield: 6 (1½-cup) servings.

FOR A QUICK MEAL: Serve with sourdough rolls and Chocolate-Berry Angel Cake (page 187).

Slim Sloppy Joe
(recipe, page 171)

Sweet-and-Spicy Bean Toss
(recipe, page 183)

Chicken Curry Wrap
(recipe, page 177)

Chicken Gumbo
(recipe, page 164)

Italian Grilled Panini
(recipe, page 170)

Cajun Jambalaya

2	regular-size bags quick-cooking boil-in-bag rice
1	teaspoon olive oil
1	(10-ounce) package frozen chopped onion, celery, and pepper seasoning blend
1	teaspoon minced garlic
½	pound 97% fat-free smoked sausage, cut into ½-inch slices (such as Lean & Hearty Hillshire Farm)
1	(14½-ounce) can Cajun-style stewed tomatoes, undrained
1	teaspoon hot sauce

POINTS

5

EXCHANGES

2 Very Lean Meat

2 Starch

1 Vegetable

PER SERVING

Calories 249

Carbohydrate 41.1g

Fat 2.8g (saturated 1.2g)

Fiber 2.3g

Protein 13.0g

Cholesterol 25mg

Sodium 996mg

Calcium 30mg

Iron 1.5mg

1. Prepare rice according to package directions, omitting salt and fat.

2. While rice cooks, heat oil in a large nonstick skillet over medium-high heat until hot. Add vegetable blend and garlic; cook 5 minutes, stirring often. Add sausage, tomatoes, and hot sauce. Bring to a boil; cover, reduce heat, and simmer 10 minutes or until thoroughly heated, stirring occasionally.

3. Spoon 1 cup rice into each individual soup bowl. Spoon tomato mixture evenly over rice. Yield: 4 servings.

 FOR A QUICK MEAL: Serve with Minted Strawberry-Pineapple Salad (page 182) and low-fat praline ice cream.

Roasted Chicken Noodle Soup

POINTS

3

EXCHANGES

2 Very Lean Meat

1½ Starch

PER SERVING

Calories 167

Carbohydrate 21.1g

Fat 1.9g (saturated 0.5g)

Fiber 0.6g

Protein 14.8g

Cholesterol 35mg

Sodium 525mg

Calcium 156mg

Iron 1.0mg

Cooking spray

2   cups frozen cubed hash brown potatoes

1½ cups frozen chopped onion, pepper, and parsley seasoning blend

2   (16-ounce) cans fat-free, low-sodium chicken broth (such as Campbell's Healthy Request)

2   ounces uncooked wide egg noodles, uncooked (about 1 cup)

½ teaspoon salt

⅛ teaspoon dried thyme

1   cup diced roasted chicken breast

1   cup evaporated skimmed milk

1. Coat a large saucepan with cooking spray; place over medium-high heat until hot. Add hash brown potatoes and seasoning blend; cook, stirring constantly, 3 minutes. Add broth and next 3 ingredients; bring to a boil. Reduce heat, and simmer, partially covered, 7 minutes. Add chicken and milk; cook 5 minutes or until noodles are tender. Yield: 5 (1-cup) servings.

FOR A QUICK MEAL: Serve with carrot sticks and saltine crackers. For the chicken, use leftover roasted chicken or pick up rotisserie chicken at your grocer's deli.

Mexican Chicken Soup

5	cups canned fat-free, low-sodium chicken broth
1½	cups thick and chunky salsa
1	(9-ounce) package frozen diced cooked chicken breast, thawed
1	cup no-salt-added black beans, rinsed and drained
1	cup instant rice, uncooked
¼	cup chopped fresh cilantro
2	tablespoons fresh lime juice
¾	cup coarsely crushed baked tortilla chips

1. Bring broth and salsa to a boil in a large, heavy saucepan over high heat. Add chicken, beans, and rice; cover, reduce heat to low, and cook 4 minutes or until rice is tender. Remove from heat; stir in cilantro and lime juice.

2. Spoon evenly into individual soup bowls. Sprinkle each serving with 2 tablespoons chips. Yield: 6 servings.

 FOR A QUICK MEAL: Serve with Creamy Corn Salad (page 183) and fresh pineapple wedges.

POINTS

5

EXCHANGES

3 Very Lean Meat

1½ Starch

PER SERVING

Calories 245

Carbohydrate 26.5g

Fat 3.6g (saturated 0.9g)

Fiber 2.5g

Protein 25.6g

Cholesterol 49mg

Sodium 816mg

Calcium 33mg

Iron 2.4mg

Chicken Gumbo *(photo, page 159)*

<u>*POINTS*</u>

3

<u>EXCHANGES</u>

2 Very Lean Meat

3 Vegetable

<u>PER SERVING</u>

Calories 164

Carbohydrate 16.8g

Fat 3.1g (saturated 0.6g)

Fiber 2.0g

Protein 16.8g

Cholesterol 33mg

Sodium 462mg

Calcium 67mg

Iron 1.1mg

1   (10-ounce) package frozen chopped onion, celery, and pepper
      seasoning blend
1   teaspoon olive oil
2   tablespoons all-purpose flour
1   cup canned reduced-sodium chicken broth
¼   teaspoon hot sauce
1   (14½-ounce) can Cajun-style stewed tomatoes, undrained
1   (10-ounce) package frozen sliced okra
1½ cups frozen diced cooked chicken breast

1. Cook frozen seasoning blend in olive oil in a large nonstick skillet over medium-high heat, stirring constantly, 3 minutes. Add flour, stirring well. Add chicken broth, hot sauce, and tomatoes; cook 3 minutes or until mixture is slightly thickened. Add okra and chicken; cover and cook 8 minutes or until okra is tender. Yield: 5 (1-cup) servings.

 FOR A QUICK MEAL: Serve with French bread and Cinnamon-Spiced Bananas (page 186).

Bagel Melts

Cooking spray
1   medium-size green pepper, sliced
1   small onion, sliced into rings
¼   teaspoon garlic powder
2   (1½-ounce) plain bagels, cut in half and toasted
2   teaspoons prepared horseradish
8   thin slices tomato (about 1 large)
8   (1-ounce) slices reduced-fat Monterey Jack cheese

1. Coat a large nonstick skillet with cooking spray; place over medium-high heat until hot. Add pepper, onion, and garlic powder; cook 4 minutes or until crisp-tender, stirring often.

2. Place bagels on a baking sheet. Spread cut side of each bagel with ½ teaspoon horseradish. Arrange 2 tomato slices on each bagel half. Spoon vegetable mixture over tomato slices. Top with cheese. Broil 3 inches from heat 2 minutes or until cheese melts. Yield: 4 servings.

POINTS
6

EXCHANGES
2 Medium-Fat Meat
1 Starch
1 Vegetable

PER SERVING
Calories 258
Carbohydrate 19.1g
Fat 11.6g (saturated 6.4g)
Fiber 2.1g
Protein 20.1g
Cholesterol 37mg
Sodium 489mg
Calcium 481mg
Iron 1.7mg

 FOR A QUICK MEAL: Serve with a bowl of creamy tomato soup or a low-fat pasta salad.

Greek Pita Rounds

POINTS

5

EXCHANGES
1 Medium-Fat Meat
2½ Starch
1 Vegetable

PER SERVING
Calories 311
Carbohydrate 56.1g
Fat 4.6g (saturated 1.9g)
Fiber 6.4g
Protein 11.5g
Cholesterol 9mg
Sodium 735mg
Calcium 151mg
Iron 3.2mg

1   (15-ounce) can garbanzo beans (chick-peas), drained
2   tablespoons fat-free milk
2   tablespoons lemon juice
3   cloves garlic
4   (8-inch) pita bread rounds
¼   cup chopped fresh parsley
2   plum tomatoes, sliced
¼   cup crumbled tomato- and basil-flavored feta cheese
¼   cup sliced ripe olives

1. Position knife blade in food processor bowl. Add first 4 ingredients; process 1 minute or until smooth, scraping sides of processor bowl occasionally.

2. Place pita rounds on a large ungreased baking sheet; spread bean mixture over pitas, leaving a ½-inch border. Arrange parsley and remaining ingredients evenly over pitas. Bake at 450° for 5 minutes or until mixture is thoroughly heated and crust is crisp. Yield: 4 servings.

FOR A QUICK MEAL: Serve with Zesty Asparagus (page 184) and sliced fresh melon.

Pinto Bean Roll-Ups

2   (15½-ounce) cans pinto beans with jalapeño peppers, rinsed
    and drained
1   cup (4 ounces) shredded reduced-fat Monterey Jack cheese
½   cup chopped green onion (about 3 medium)
6   (8-inch) fat-free whole wheat flour tortillas
Cooking spray
¼   cup plus 2 tablespoons salsa
3   tablespoons nonfat sour cream

1. Place beans in a small bowl; slightly mash with back of a fork.
Add cheese and green onions, stirring well.

2. Spread bean mixture evenly in centers of tortillas; fold in sides,
and roll up. Place tortillas, seam side down, on a baking sheet
coated with cooking spray. Bake at 350° for 10 minutes or until
thoroughly heated. Top each roll-up with 1 tablespoon salsa and
1½ teaspoons sour cream. Yield: 6 servings.

FOR A QUICK MEAL: Serve with Lemon-Pepper Corn on
the Cob (page 184) and fresh fruit salad.

POINTS
4

EXCHANGES
1 Medium-Fat Meat
3 Starch
1 Vegetable

PER SERVING
Calories 330
Carbohydrate 53.3g
Fat 4.9g (saturated 2.1g)
Fiber 14.9g
Protein 18.5g
Cholesterol 12mg
Sodium 738mg
Calcium 164mg
Iron 0.4mg

Couscous-Tabbouleh Pitas

POINTS

6

EXCHANGES

1 Medium-Fat Meat

3 Starch

1 Vegetable

PER SERVING

Calories 330

Carbohydrate 57.6g

Fat 6.8g (saturated 2.1g)

Fiber 3.8g

Protein 11.3g

Cholesterol 10mg

Sodium 581mg

Calcium 124mg

Iron 2.9mg

¾ cup water

½ cup couscous, uncooked

2 large tomatoes

⅓ cup chopped fresh parsley

⅓ cup crumbled tomato- and basil-flavored feta cheese

¼ cup sliced green onions

¼ cup commercial reduced-fat olive oil-flavored vinaigrette

4 leaves green leaf lettuce

4 (6-inch) pita bread rounds, cut in half

1. Bring water to a boil in a small saucepan; add couscous. Cover and remove from heat. Let stand 5 minutes.

2. While couscous stands, coarsely chop tomatoes (to make about 2½ cups). Fluff couscous with a fork. Combine couscous, chopped tomato, parsley, and next 3 ingredients. Place 1 lettuce leaf into each pita half; spoon couscous mixture evenly into pita halves. Yield: 4 servings.

FOR A QUICK MEAL: Serve with Sliced Melon with Raspberry Sauce (page 182).

Green Chile-Beef Wraps

1½ cups packaged shredded cabbage
¼ cup chopped fresh cilantro
¼ teaspoon ground cumin
½ cup green chile salsa
4   (7-inch) fat-free flour tortillas
6   ounces thinly sliced deli roast beef
Butter-flavored cooking spray
¼ cup shredded reduced-fat Monterey Jack cheese
¼ cup nonfat sour cream

POINTS

4

EXCHANGES

2 Very Lean Meat

1½ Starch

1 Vegetable

PER SERVING

Calories 214

Carbohydrate 28.8g

Fat 3.1g (saturated 1.5g)

Fiber 1.9g

Protein 16.3g

Cholesterol 27mg

Sodium 892mg

Calcium 76mg

Iron 1.9mg

1. Combine cabbage and cilantro in a medium bowl. Stir cumin into salsa; stir salsa mixture into cabbage mixture.

2. Place tortillas on a damp paper towel in microwave oven; cover with another damp paper towel. Microwave at HIGH 40 seconds to 1 minute or until warm.

3. Spoon cabbage mixture evenly down centers of tortillas. Top evenly with roast beef. Roll up tortillas; place, seam side down, in an 11- x 7- x 1½-inch baking dish coated with cooking spray. Coat tortillas with cooking spray; cover and bake at 450° for 15 minutes or until thoroughly heated. Sprinkle with cheese.

4. Place on individual serving plates. Top each wrap with 1 table-spoon sour cream. Yield: 4 servings.

 FOR A QUICK MEAL: Serve with low-fat vanilla ice cream topped with sliced strawberries.

Italian Grilled Panini *(photo, page 160)*

POINTS

6

EXCHANGES

2 Lean Meat

2 Starch

1 Vegetable

PER SERVING

Calories 272

Carbohydrate 36.7g

Fat 6.2g (saturated 2.3g)

Fiber 2.0g

Protein 19.6g

Cholesterol 30mg

Sodium 846mg

Calcium 295mg

Iron 2.1mg

8   (1-ounce) slices Vienna bread

6   ounces sliced reduced-sodium deli smoked ham

4   (¾-ounce) slices reduced-fat provolone cheese or part-skim
    mozzarella cheese

1   (7-ounce) jar roasted red pepper, cut into strips

Garlic-flavored cooking spray

1. Top 4 bread slices with ham, cheese, and pepper strips; top with remaining bread slices.

2. Coat both sides of sandwiches with cooking spray. Place sandwiches on an ungreased baking sheet. Bake at 450° for 5 minutes on each side or until bread is golden and cheese is melted. Yield: 4 servings.

 FOR A QUICK MEAL: Serve with Romaine and Apple Salad (page 182).

Slim Sloppy Joes *(photo, page 157)*

1	pound lean ground round	
1	cup chopped onion	
¼	cup reduced-calorie ketchup	
2	tablespoons unprocessed oat bran	
1	tablespoon low-sodium Worcestershire sauce	
1	tablespoon prepared mustard	
1	tablespoon lemon juice	
1	(8-ounce) can no-salt-added tomato sauce	
6	reduced-calorie hamburger buns, split and toasted	

1. Cook ground round and onion in a large nonstick skillet over medium-high heat until meat is browned, stirring until meat crumbles. Drain and return to skillet.

2. Stir ketchup and next 5 ingredients into meat mixture; bring to a boil. Cover, reduce heat, and simmer 10 minutes, stirring often. Spoon mixture evenly over bottom halves of buns; cover with bun tops. Yield: 6 servings.

 FOR A QUICK MEAL: Serve with Sweet-and-Spicy Bean Toss (page 183) and a glass of fat-free milk.

POINTS

4

EXCHANGES

2 Lean Meat

1½ Starch

PER SERVING

Calories 226

Carbohydrate 27.3g

Fat 5.3g (saturated 1.7g)

Fiber 5.6g

Protein 21.2g

Cholesterol 46mg

Sodium 319mg

Calcium 10mg

Iron 2.1mg

Spicy Beef Sandwiches

POINTS

3

EXCHANGES

2 Very Lean Meat

1½ Starch

1 Vegetable

PER SERVING

Calories 198

Carbohydrate 28.0g

Fat 4.2g (saturated 1.3g)

Fiber 6.9g

Protein 17.4g

Cholesterol 35mg

Sodium 693mg

Calcium 61mg

Iron 2.4mg

¾   pound ground round
Cooking spray
1½ cups green pepper strips
1   (14½-ounce) can no-salt-added Mexican-style stewed
        tomatoes, undrained
2   tablespoons reduced-sodium soy sauce
1   teaspoon ground ginger
½   teaspoon dried crushed red pepper
¼   cup minced fresh cilantro
6   reduced-calorie whole wheat hamburger buns

1. Cook ground round in a large nonstick skillet over medium-high heat until browned, stirring until it crumbles. Drain and pat dry with a paper towel. Wipe drippings from skillet with a paper towel.

2. Coat skillet with cooking spray; add green pepper, and cook over medium-high heat 4 minutes or until tender. Stir in beef, tomatoes, and next 3 ingredients. Bring to a boil; reduce heat, and simmer, uncovered, 4 to 5 minutes or until most of liquid is evaporated. Stir in cilantro.

3. Spoon ½ cup beef mixture over bottom half of each bun. Cover with bun tops. Yield: 6 servings.

 FOR A QUICK MEAL: Serve with Quick-Roasted Sweet Potatoes (page 185) and sliced pears.

Steak and Onion Sandwiches

2	teaspoons bottled minced garlic
½	teaspoon dried thyme
½	teaspoon dried basil
½	teaspoon freshly ground pepper
1	(1-pound) flank steak, trimmed
4	¼-inch slices purple onion
Cooking spray	
3	tablespoons nonfat mayonnaise
2½	teaspoons Dijon mustard
8	(1-ounce) slices sourdough bread, toasted

POINTS

8

EXCHANGES

3 Medium-Fat Meat

2 Starch

PER SERVING

Calories 370

Carbohydrate 30.6g

Fat 14.6g (saturated 5.6g)

Fiber 1.3g

Protein 27.6g

Cholesterol 61mg

Sodium 549mg

Calcium 76mg

Iron 4.1mg

1. Combine first 4 ingredients; rub mixture over steak. Place a nonstick skillet over medium-high heat until hot. Coat steak and onion slices with cooking spray; add steak and onion to skillet. Cook 12 minutes or to desired degree of doneness, stirring onion often and turning steak once.

2. Combine mayonnaise and mustard, stirring well; spread over 1 side of each bread slice. Thinly slice steak across the grain. Arrange steak evenly on 4 bread slices; top evenly with onion. Top with remaining bread slices. Yield: 4 servings.

 FOR A QUICK MEAL: Serve with Maple-Glazed Carrots (page 184).

Cajun Shrimp Po' Boy

POINTS

5

EXCHANGES

3 Very Lean Meat

2 Starch

PER SERVING

Calories 247

Carbohydrate 29.5g

Fat 3.0g (saturated 0.7g)

Fiber 1.6g

Protein 23.3g

Cholesterol 166mg

Sodium 554mg

Calcium 77mg

Iron 3.9mg

1   pound peeled, deveined large fresh shrimp
3   tablespoons lemon juice
⅓   cup nonfat sour cream
3   tablespoons reduced-sodium dill pickle relish (such as
        Cascadian Farms)
3   drops of hot sauce
1   tablespoon no-salt-added Creole seasoning
Cooking spray
4   (1.7-ounce) French rolls, split lengthwise

1. Place shrimp in a shallow dish, and drizzle with lemon juice; let stand at room temperature 5 minutes.

2. Combine sour cream, relish, and hot sauce in a small bowl, stirring well; cover tartar sauce, and chill.

3. Drain shrimp on paper towels, discarding lemon juice. Sprinkle both sides of shrimp with Creole seasoning; thread shrimp evenly onto five 12-inch skewers. Coat grill rack with cooking spray; place rack over medium-hot coals (350° to 400°). Grill, covered, 3 minutes on each side or until shrimp turn pink.

4. While shrimp grill, place rolls, split side down, on grill rack; grill 2 minutes or until lightly toasted; keep warm.

5. Remove shrimp from skewers; place evenly on warm rolls. Serve with chilled tartar sauce. Yield: 4 servings.

 FOR A QUICK MEAL: Serve with sliced tomatoes and Butterscotch Syrup Cake (page 187).

Dilled Chicken Salad Sandwiches

½   cup plain nonfat yogurt
2   cups chopped cooked chicken (cooked without salt or fat)
¼   cup chopped celery
¼   cup chopped green onions
1   tablespoon honey mustard
¼   teaspoon dried dillweed
¼   teaspoon ground white pepper
4   leaves green leaf lettuce
8   (1-ounce) slices whole wheat bread, lightly toasted
4   (¼-inch-thick) slices large tomato

1. Spoon yogurt onto several layers of heavy-duty paper towels, and spread to ½-inch thickness. Cover with additional paper towels; let stand 5 minutes. Scrape yogurt into a medium bowl, using a rubber spatula.

2. Add chicken and next 5 ingredients to yogurt; stir well. Place lettuce leaves over 4 bread slices; top with chicken mixture, tomato slices, and remaining bread slices. Yield: 4 servings.

POINTS
6

EXCHANGES
3 Lean Meat
2 Starch

PER SERVING
Calories 323
Carbohydrate 34.5g
Fat 7.8g (saturated 2.0g)
Fiber 3.5g
Protein 28.1g
Cholesterol 64mg
Sodium 410mg
Calcium 143mg
Iron 3.3mg

 FOR A QUICK MEAL: Serve with low-fat cream of broccoli soup.

Greek Chicken Tortilla Wraps

POINTS
6

EXCHANGES
3 Lean Meat
1½ Starch
1 Vegetable

PER SERVING
Calories 324
Carbohydrate 29.4g
Fat 11.3g (saturated 4.3g)
Fiber 8.2g
Protein 27.1g
Cholesterol 60mg
Sodium 636mg
Calcium 180mg
Iron 3.3mg

4   (8-inch) fat-free whole wheat flour tortillas
3   tablespoons finely chopped walnuts·
1   teaspoon olive oil
1   (9-ounce) package frozen cooked chicken strips
1   teaspoon minced garlic
1   (10-ounce) package prewashed fresh spinach, rinsed
½   teaspoon no-salt-added Greek seasoning
3   ounces crumbled feta cheese

1. Wrap tortillas in aluminum foil; bake at 350° for 10 minutes.

2. While tortillas bake, place a nonstick skillet over medium heat until hot. Add walnuts; cook, shaking pan often, 3 minutes or until walnuts are lightly browned. Remove walnuts from skillet; set aside.

3. Heat oil in skillet over medium-high heat. Add chicken and garlic; cook 1 minute. Add half of spinach; cover and cook 3 minutes or until spinach wilts. Add remaining spinach; cover and cook 2 minutes to wilt. Sprinkle with Greek seasoning, and toss gently.

4. Sprinkle cheese and walnuts evenly down centers of tortillas. Spoon chicken and spinach mixture over cheese mixture. Roll up tortillas. Place, seam side down, on individual serving plates; cut in half, if desired. Yield: 4 servings.

 FOR A QUICK MEAL: Serve with Greek Rice (page 185) and sliced plums.

Chicken Curry Wraps *(photo, page 158)*

2	cups shredded skinned rotisserie chicken
¼	cup mango chutney
2	tablespoons nonfat mayonnaise
2	tablespoons golden raisins
1	teaspoon curry powder
4	(8-inch) flour tortillas
½	cup chopped radish
½	cup chopped broccoli
½	cup alfalfa sprouts

POINTS

7

EXCHANGES

3 Lean Meat

2 Starch

1 Vegetable

PER SERVING

Calories 329

Carbohydrate 40.8g

Fat 8.9g (saturated 1.4g)

Fiber 2.0g

Protein 22.5g

Cholesterol 126mg

Sodium 448mg

Calcium 76mg

Iron 1.8mg

1. Combine first 5 ingredients, stirring well. Cover and chill, if desired.

2. Wrap tortillas loosely in wax paper; microwave at HIGH 30 seconds or just until softened. Spoon chicken mixture evenly down centers of tortillas; top with radish, broccoli, and sprouts. Roll up tortillas. Yield: 4 servings.

 FOR A QUICK MEAL: Serve with Asian Coleslaw (page 183) and orange sections.

Italian Chicken Subs

EXCHANGES
4 Very Lean Meat
2 Starch
1 Vegetable

PER SERVING
Calories 345
Carbohydrate 42.0g
Fat 4.2g (saturated 1.4g)
Fiber 2.4g
Protein 35.9g
Cholesterol 68mg
Sodium 916mg
Calcium 152mg
Iron 2.8mg

4   reduced-fat Philly-style hoagie rolls (such as Cobblestone), split lengthwise
3   tablespoons nonfat mayonnaise
¼   teaspoon dried Italian seasoning
Cooking spray
1   pound chicken breast tenders
2   tablespoons low-sodium soy sauce
2   (¾-ounce) fat-free Swiss cheese singles
1   (7-ounce) jar roasted red peppers, drained and sliced
½   medium-size green pepper, sliced

1. Place rolls, cut side up, on a baking sheet; spread mayonnaise evenly over rolls. Sprinkle with Italian seasoning. Bake at 400° for 3 to 5 minutes or until lightly browned.

2. Coat a large nonstick skillet with cooking spray; place over medium-high heat. Add chicken and soy sauce; cook 6 to 7 minutes or until chicken is done, stirring often.

3. Meanwhile, cut cheese slices in half; place a half slice on each sandwich. Spoon red and green peppers evenly over cheese. Top with chicken and hoagie roll tops. Yield: 4 servings.

 FOR A QUICK MEAL: Serve with carrot sticks and baked potato chips.

Hickory-Grilled Chicken Sandwiches

Cooking spray
4   (4-ounce) boneless, skinless chicken breast halves
4   (¼-inch-thick) slices purple onion
⅓   cup hickory-flavored barbecue sauce
4   canned pineapple slices
4   reduced-calorie hamburger buns

POINTS

5

EXCHANGES

3 Very Lean Meat

1 ½ Starch

½ Fruit

1. Coat grill rack with cooking spray; place on grill over medium-hot coals (350° to 400°). Brush chicken and onion with barbecue sauce. Place chicken, onion, and pineapple on grill rack; grill, covered, 5 minutes on each side or until a meat thermometer inserted in thickest part of breast registers 170°, removing onion and pineapple when tender.

2. Place each chicken breast on a bottom half of bun; top with onion, pineapple, and top half of bun. Yield: 4 servings.

PER SERVING

Calories 276

Carbohydrate 30.3g

Fat 4.4g (saturated 1.0g)

Fiber 3.8g

Protein 30.2g

Cholesterol 70mg

Sodium 421mg

Calcium 55mg

Iron 2.5mg

FOR A QUICK MEAL: Serve with Minted Peas (page 185) and watermelon wedges or frozen melon balls.

Smoky Slaw Dogs

POINTS

5

EXCHANGES

2 Very Lean Meat

2 Starch

1 Vegetable

PER SERVING

Calories 248

Carbohydrate 38.9g

Fat 4.4g (saturated 1.1g)

Fiber 2.3g

Protein 12.6g

Cholesterol 23mg

Sodium 872mg

Calcium 89mg

Iron 1.8mg

¼   cup sugar

¼   cup cider vinegar

2   tablespoons water

1   teaspoon spicy brown mustard

½   teaspoon celery seeds

Dash of pepper

4   cups packaged coleslaw mix

1   (14-ounce) package low-fat smoked turkey sausage (such as Healthy Choice)

2   tablespoons spicy brown mustard

6   hot dog buns, split and toasted

1. Combine first 6 ingredients in a nonstick skillet; bring to a boil. Reduce heat, and simmer, stirring often until sugar dissolves. Stir in coleslaw, and cook until cabbage wilts. Remove from skillet, and keep warm.

2. Cut sausages in half lengthwise; cut each half into 3 pieces (to make 12 pieces total). Place skillet over medium heat until hot; add sausage, and cook until browned and thoroughly heated, turning occasionally.

3. Spread 2 tablespoons mustard evenly over split sides of buns; place 2 sausage pieces in each bun. Spoon coleslaw mixture evenly over sausage, using a slotted spoon. Yield: 6 servings.

 FOR A QUICK MEAL: Serve with fat-free baked beans and Melon Boat with Frozen Yogurt (page 186).

added attractions

These recipes have just five ingredients (or less),
making them a snap to prepare. The best part?
POINTS per serving range from 0 to a mere 5!

Easy Salads

1 • Sliced Melon with Raspberry Sauce

Thaw 1 (10-ounce) package frozen unsweetened raspberries. Process thawed raspberries, 2 table-spoons raspberry vinegar, and 4 teaspoons honey in an electric blender until smooth; pour through a wire-mesh strainer to remove seeds. Peel and slice 1 small cantaloupe. Arrange 10 Boston lettuce leaves and cantaloupe slices evenly on five salad plates. Drizzle with raspberry sauce. Sprinkle with 2 tablespoons chopped fresh mint. Yield: 5 servings.

POINTS: 1 ▪ EXCHANGES: 1½ Fruit ▪
PER SERVING: Calories 99, Carbohydrate 24.2g,
Fat 0.8g, Fiber 6.0g, Protein 2.0g

2 • Minted Strawberry-Pineapple Salad

Combine 1 cup quartered fresh strawberries, 1 cup fresh pineapple chunks, and ¾ teaspoon dried mint flakes; toss well. Pour ¼ cup fat-free poppy seed dressing over fruit; toss gently. Place 1 green lettuce leaf on each salad plate. Top with fruit mixture. Yield: 2 servings.

POINTS: 2 ▪ EXCHANGES: 1½ Fruit ▪
PER SERVING: Calories 111, Carbohydrate 24.9g,
Fat 0.7g, Fiber 3.4g, Protein 2.0g

3 • Romaine and Apple Salad

Arrange 4 cups loosely packed packaged torn romaine lettuce evenly on four salad plates. Thinly slice 1 Red Delicious apple; fan apple slices over lettuce. Sprinkle with 1½ tablespoons chopped pecans. Whisk together ¼ cup fat-free balsamic vinaigrette dressing and ⅛ teaspoon garlic powder; drizzle over salads. Yield: 4 servings.

POINTS: 1 ▪ EXCHANGES: 1 Vegetable, ½ Fruit ▪
PER SERVING: Calories 78, Carbohydrate 14.0g,
Fat 2.7g, Fiber 2.6g, Protein 0.9g

4 • Fruited Spinach Salad

Thaw ⅓ cup frozen orange juice concentrate. Combine orange juice concentrate, ⅔ cup nonfat mayonnaise, and ¼ cup water. Arrange 1 (10-ounce) package fresh washed and trimmed spinach evenly on six salad plates. Arrange 3 thinly sliced pears evenly over salads; sprinkle with ¼ cup coarsely chopped toasted pecans. Drizzle salads with dressing. Yield: 6 servings.

POINTS: 2 ▪ EXCHANGES: 1 Vegetable, ½ Fruit, 1 Fat ▪
PER SERVING: Calories 146, Carbohydrate 28.2g,
Fat 4.0g, Fiber 4.5g, Protein 2.5g

5 • Asian Coleslaw

Drain 1 (11-ounce) can mandarin oranges in light syrup, reserving 2 tablespoons syrup; combine syrup and ½ cup fat-free toasted sesame salad dressing. Combine oranges, 4 cups shredded cabbage, 2 cups fresh bean sprouts, and 3 tablespoons chopped cashews. Add dressing; toss gently. Yield: 14 (½-cup) servings.

POINTS: 1 • EXCHANGE: 1 Vegetable •
PER SERVING: Calories 39, Carbohydrate 7.1g,
Fat 0.9g, Fiber 0.8g, Protein 1.0g

6 • Asparagus Salad with Blue Cheese

Snap tough ends off 1 pound fresh asparagus. Steam asparagus 4 minutes. Plunge into ice water; drain. Arrange 2 lettuce leaves on each of four salad plates; top with asparagus. Combine ¼ cup lemon juice and 3 tablespoons fat-free raspberry vinaigrette; drizzle over salads. Sprinkle evenly with ¼ cup blue cheese. Yield: 4 servings.

POINTS: 2 • EXCHANGES: 2 Vegetable, 1 Fat •
PER SERVING: Calories 93, Carbohydrate 10.2g,
Fat 4.3g, Fiber 2.3g, Protein 5.6g

7 • Sweet-and-Spicy Bean Toss

Rinse and drain 1 (19-ounce) can garbanzo beans and 1 (16-ounce) can dark red kidney beans. Drain 1 (14½-ounce) can no-salt-added cut green beans. Combine beans in a bowl. Combine ⅓ cup fat-free Catalina dressing, 1½ tablespoons cider vinegar, and ¼ teaspoon ground red pepper; toss with bean mixture. Yield: 11 (½-cup) servings.

POINTS: 1 • EXCHANGE: 1 Starch •
PER SERVING: Calories 83, Carbohydrate 15.7g,
Fat 0.5g, Fiber 3.7g, Protein 4.9g

8 • Creamy Corn Salad

Rinse 2 cups frozen whole-kernel yellow corn with warm water until thawed; drain. Place corn in a bowl; stir in ½ cup chopped sweet red pepper, ⅓ cup sliced green onions, ¼ cup nonfat mayonnaise, 1 tablespoon vinegar, and ¼ teaspoon no-salt-added Creole seasoning. Yield: 4 servings.

POINTS: 2 • EXCHANGES: 1 Starch, 1 Vegetable •
PER SERVING: Calories 102, Carbohydrate 24.2g,
Fat 0.8g, Fiber 2.8g, Protein 3.1g

9 • Greek Vegetable Salad

Combine 2 cups halved cherry tomatoes, 1 cup chopped cucumber, and ¼ cup fat-free balsamic vinaigrette; toss. Add ¼ cup crumbled garlic- and herb-flavored feta cheese and 2 tablespoons chopped fresh parsley. Place 1 red leaf lettuce leaf on each of eight salad plates; top evenly with tomato mixture and 8 kalamata olives. Sprinkle with ground pepper, if desired. Yield: 4 servings.

POINTS: 1 • EXCHANGES: 1 Vegetable, 1 Fat •
PER SERVING: Calories 61, Carbohydrate 9.7g,
Fat 2.7g, Fiber 2.0g, Protein 2.6g

10 • Italian Antipasto Salad

Toss together the following ingredients: 6 cups packaged salad mix; 1 (14-ounce) can quartered artichoke hearts, drained; 1 small zucchini, thinly sliced; ⅓ cup bottled roasted red peppers in water, cut into thin strips; 2 tablespoons grated Parmesan cheese; ¼ teaspoon ground pepper; and ⅓ cup fat-free Italian dressing. Yield: 4 servings.

POINTS: 1 • EXCHANGES: 2 Vegetable •
PER SERVING: Calories 72, Carbohydrate 11.5g,
Fat 1.5g, Fiber 1.3g, Protein 4.9g

Speedy Sides

1 · Zesty Asparagus

Snap off tough ends of 1 pound fresh asparagus. Place asparagus and 2 tablespoons water in a baking dish; cover and microwave at HIGH 5 minutes, turning dish once. Drain asparagus, and place on a serving platter. Combine 2 tablespoons fat-free Italian dressing, 1 tablespoon balsamic vinegar, and $1/4$ teaspoon minced garlic; drizzle over asparagus. Yield: 4 servings.

POINTS: 0 ▪ EXCHANGE: 1 Vegetable ▪
PER SERVING: Calories 27, Carbohydrate 5.1g,
Fat 0.3g, Fiber 1.0g, Protein 2.6g

2 · Blue Cheese Green Beans

Place 1 pound fresh green beans and 2 tablespoons water in an 11- x 7- x $1^1/2$-inch microwave-safe dish. Cover and microwave at HIGH 10 to 12 minutes or until tender; drain. Transfer beans to a serving dish; toss with $1^1/2$ teaspoons balsamic vinegar, $1/2$ teaspoon olive oil, and 2 tablespoons crumbled blue cheese. Yield: 4 servings.

POINTS: 1 ▪ EXCHANGES: 1 Vegetable, $1/2$ Fat ▪
PER SERVING: Calories 62, Carbohydrate 7.5g,
Fat 2.7g, Fiber 2.2g, Protein 3.4g

3 · Maple-Glazed Carrots

Place $1^1/2$ cups sliced carrot, 2 tablespoons reduced-calorie maple syrup, 1 teaspoon margarine, and $1/4$ teaspoon salt-free herb-and-spice blend in a small microwave-safe bowl. Cover and microwave at HIGH 6 to 8 minutes or until tender, stirring every 2 minutes. Yield: 2 servings.

POINTS: 1 ▪ EXCHANGES: 2 Vegetable ▪
PER SERVING: Calories 66, Carbohydrate 12.1g,
Fat 2.1g, Fiber 3.2g, Protein 1.0g

4 · Lemon-Pepper Corn on the Cob

Coat 4 ears corn with butter-flavored cooking spray, and sprinkle with $1/2$ teaspoon salt-free lemon-pepper seasoning. Arrange corn in a circle on a round microwave-safe platter with thicker ends of cobs toward outside of circle. Cover loosely with wax paper. Microwave at HIGH 8 minutes or until corn is tender, turning after 4 minutes. Yield: 4 servings.

POINTS: 1 ▪ EXCHANGE: 1 Starch ▪
PER SERVING: Calories 41, Carbohydrate 8.8g,
Fat 0.7g, Fiber 1.5g, Protein 1.5g

5 • Mushroom and Pepper Skillet

Slice 1 large sweet red pepper into strips. Coat a nonstick skillet with cooking spray; place over medium-high heat until hot. Add pepper strips, 1 (8-ounce) package sliced fresh mushrooms, $\frac{1}{4}$ teaspoon dried rosemary, and 1 tablespoon low-sodium soy sauce. Cover; cook 4 minutes. Stir well; cover and cook 3 more minutes or until crisp-tender. Yield: 2 ($\frac{2}{3}$-cup) servings.

POINTS: 1 • EXCHANGES: 2 Vegetable •
PER SERVING: Calories 48, Carbohydrate 7.9g,
Fat 1.1g, Fiber 2.3g, Protein 2.8g

6 • Minted Peas

Cook 1 (9-ounce) package frozen baby sweet peas according to package directions; transfer to a serving bowl. Add 1 teaspoon margarine and 1 teaspoon dried mint flakes; toss lightly, and serve immediately. Yield: 3 ($\frac{1}{2}$-cup) servings.

POINTS: 1 • EXCHANGE: 1 Starch •
PER SERVING: Calories 81, Carbohydrate 13.0g,
Fat 1.3g, Fiber 4.0g, Protein 4.0g

7 • Rosemary Potatoes

Cut 2 large baking potatoes into $\frac{1}{4}$-inch-thick slices. Place potato in a large serving bowl; add 2 teaspoons reduced-sodium soy sauce, 1 teaspoon olive oil, $\frac{1}{4}$ teaspoon dried rosemary, and $\frac{1}{4}$ teaspoon salt. Toss well. Cover with heavy-duty plastic wrap, and vent. Microwave at HIGH 12 minutes or potatoes are tender, stirring every 4 minutes. Yield: 4 servings.

POINTS: 2 • EXCHANGES: 1½ Starch •
PER SERVING: Calories 117, Carbohydrate 23.9g,
Fat 1.3g, Fiber 2.3g, Protein 3.3g

8 • Quick-Roasted Sweet Potatoes

Peel 1 large sweet potato; cut into 1-inch cubes. Spread cubes on a baking sheet coated with cooking spray. Bake at 450° for 15 minutes.

Meanwhile, combine 1 tablespoon molasses, $\frac{1}{4}$ teaspoon ground cinnamon, and 2 tablespoons orange juice. Transfer sweet potato to a serving bowl. Pour molasses mixture over potato; toss gently. Yield: 2 (1-cup) servings.

POINTS: 4 • EXCHANGES: 3 Starch •
PER SERVING: Calories 227, Carbohydrate 52.4g,
Fat 0.7g, Fiber 3.5g, Protein 3.8g

9 • Parmesan Broiled Tomatoes

Cut 2 medium tomatoes into 4 slices each; place on an ovenproof platter. Combine 2 tablespoons fat-free Italian dressing and $\frac{1}{2}$ teaspoon salt-free herb-and-spice blend; drizzle over tomato slices. Sprinkle with 2 tablespoons grated Parmesan cheese. Broil 3 inches from heat 3 minutes. Yield: 3 servings.

POINTS: 1 • EXCHANGE: 1 Vegetable •
PER SERVING: Calories 38, Carbohydrate 5.5g,
Fat 1.3g, Fiber 1.1g, Protein 2.1g

10 • Greek Rice

Cook 1 package boil-in-bag rice according to package directions, omitting salt and fat. Drain. Place in a serving bowl; add 1 cup chopped tomato, $1\frac{1}{2}$ tablespoons chopped ripe olives, 1 tablespoon lemon juice, and $\frac{1}{2}$ teaspoon salt-free Greek seasoning. Toss. Yield: 3 ($\frac{3}{4}$-cup) servings.

POINTS: 3 • EXCHANGES: 2 Starch •
PER SERVING: Calories 136, Carbohydrate 29.8g,
Fat 0.6g, Fiber 1.3g, Protein 2.7g

Quick Desserts

---

1 • Apple Pie Sundae

Melt 1 tablespoon margarine in a large nonstick skillet; add 2 cups peeled apple slices, ¼ cup firmly packed brown sugar, and ½ teaspoon ground nutmeg. Cook over medium-high heat 6 minutes or until apple is tender. For each serving, spoon ¼ cup apple slices over ½ cup nonfat vanilla ice cream. Drizzle each serving with 1 teaspoon fat-free caramel topping. Yield: 4 servings.

POINTS: 4 • EXCHANGES: 1½ Starch, 1 Fruit, 1 Fat • PER SERVING: Calories 224, Carbohydrate 48.1g, Fat 3.2g, Fiber 1.7g, Protein 5.2g

2 • Cinnamon-Spiced Bananas

Slice 2 large bananas; place banana in a 1-quart microwave-safe casserole. Sprinkle 2 tablespoons brown sugar, ¼ teaspoon ground cinnamon, and ½ teaspoon vanilla extract over bananas; dot with 2 teaspoons margarine. Cover with heavy-duty plastic wrap, and vent. Microwave at HIGH 1 to 2 minutes or until sugar melts, stirring once.

Spoon ½ cup ice cream into each of four individual bowls; spoon banana mixture evenly over ice cream. Serve immediately. Yield: 4 servings.

POINTS: 4 • EXCHANGES: 1½ Starch, 1 Fruit • PER SERVING: Calories 192, Carbohydrate 39.9g, Fat 2.1g, Fiber 1.5g, Protein 5.5g

3 • Citrus with Granola Crunch

Spread 1 cup low-fat granola with raisins in a shallow pan; dot with 1 tablespoon margarine. Sprinkle with 1 tablespoon brown sugar. Broil 3 inches from heat 2 to 3 minutes or until toasted, stirring often.

Combine 1 cup refrigerated orange slices and 1 cup refrigerated grapefruit slices. Spoon into four bowls. Sprinkle each serving with ¼ cup granola mixture. Top each with 2 tablespoons nonfat vanilla frozen yogurt. Yield: 4 servings.

POINTS: 4 • EXCHANGES: 1½ Starch, 1 Fruit, 1 Fat • PER SERVING: Calories 206, Carbohydrate 39.2g, Fat 4.5g, Fiber 2.1g, Protein 3.2g

4 • Melon Boat with Frozen Yogurt

Peel ½ large cantaloupe; cut melon lengthwise into 4 wedges. Fill each wedge with ¼ cup nonfat vanilla-raspberry frozen yogurt; sprinkle each serving with 1 teaspoon toasted flaked coconut. Serve immediately. Yield: 4 servings.

POINTS: 2 • EXCHANGE: 1 Fruit • PER SERVING: Calories 83, Carbohydrate 17.6g, Fat 0.9g, Fiber 0.7g, Protein 2.7g

5 • Peachy Parfaits

Drain 1 (15-ounce) can peach slices in light syrup; coarsely chop peaches. Alternate layers of peaches and 2 (8-ounce) cartons vanilla low-fat yogurt in four parfait glasses, beginning with fruit and ending with yogurt. Sprinkle each with $1\frac{1}{2}$ teaspoons brown sugar. Cut 4 gingersnaps in half; place 2 halves on each parfait. Yield: 4 servings.

POINTS: 4 • EXCHANGES: ½ Skim Milk, 1 Starch, 1 Fruit •
PER SERVING: Calories 183, Carbohydrate 34.7g, Fat 2.8g, Fiber 0.2g, Protein 6.4g

6 • Strawberry Trifle

Tear 6 ounces angel food cake into bite-size pieces; place half of cake pieces in a 1-quart glass bowl. Drizzle with 1 teaspoon light rum. Slightly mash 1 (10-ounce) package frozen strawberries. Place half of strawberries over cake pieces. Spread 1 cup thawed frozen reduced-calorie whipped topping over strawberries. Top with remaining cake pieces, 1 teaspoon light rum, remaining strawberries, and $\frac{1}{2}$ cup whipped topping. Yield: 6 servings.

POINTS: 3 • EXCHANGES: 1 Starch, ½ Fruit •
PER SERVING: Calories 133, Carbohydrate 24.8g, Fat 2.3g, Fiber 0.4g, Protein 2.4g

7 • Chocolate-Berry Angel Cake

Place 4 ($1\frac{1}{2}$-inch-thick) slices angel food cake on individual dessert plates. Top each with $\frac{1}{4}$ cup fat-free strawberry ice cream, $\frac{1}{2}$ cup sliced strawberries, and 1 tablespoon warm fat-free fudge sauce. Yield: 4 servings.

POINTS: 4 • EXCHANGES: 3 Starch •
PER SERVING: Calories 253, Carbohydrate 58.3g, Fat 0.6g, Fiber 4.4g, Protein 6.1g

8 • Butterscotch Syrup Cake

Place 4 ($\frac{3}{4}$-inch-thick) slices fat-free light golden loaf cake on individual dessert plates. Heat $\frac{1}{4}$ cup fat-free butterscotch sundae syrup. Toast 3 tablespoons chopped pecans in a small skillet. Top each slice cake with 2 tablespoons frozen reduced-fat whipped topping, and drizzle each with 1 tablespoon syrup. Sprinkle evenly with pecans. Yield: 4 servings.

POINTS: 4 • EXCHANGES: 2 Starch, 1 Fat •
PER SERVING: Calories 182, Carbohydrate 30.6g, Fat 5.3g, Fiber 0.7g, Protein 2.0g

9 • Strawberry-Amaretto Smoothie

Combine 1 cup fat-free milk and 3 tablespoons amaretto in an electric blender. With blender running, remove center cap from cover, and slowly drop 3 cups frozen strawberries into milk mixture; process until smooth. Add 2 cups nonfat strawberry frozen yogurt; process until smooth, stopping as necessary to scrape sides. Serve immediately. Yield: 4 (1-cup) servings.

POINTS: 3 • EXCHANGES: 1 Starch, 1 Fruit •
PER SERVING: Calories 168, Carbohydrate 29.3g, Fat 1.7g, Fiber 0.9g, Protein 4.7g

10 • Dreamy Orange Smoothie

Process 2 cups orange sherbet, 2 cups low-fat vanilla ice cream, and $\frac{1}{2}$ cup low-fat milk in an electric blender until thick and smooth. Pour into glasses, and serve immediately. Yield: 4 (1-cup) servings.

POINTS: 5 • EXCHANGES: 2½ Starch •
PER SERVING: Calories 217, Carbohydrate 36.9g, Fat 6.0g, Fiber 0.0g, Protein 4.8g

Recipe Index

Acknowledgments

Cyclamen Studio, Inc., Berkeley, CA
Daisy Hill, Louisville, KY
Dish, Boston, MA
DYOA, Portland, OR
E&M Glass, Cheshire, UK
Eigen Arts, Inc., Jersey City, NJ
Alice Goldsmith, New York, NY
Judy Jackson, New York, NY
Marge Margulies, Philadelphia, PA
Pastis & Co., New York, NY

Rina Peleg, Brooklyn, NY
Pillivyt-Franmara, Salinas, CA
Jill Rosenwald, Boston, MA
Smyer Glass, Benicia, CA
Union Street Glass, Oakland, CA
Vietri, Hillsborough, NC

Sources of Nutrient Analysis Data:
Computrition, Inc., Chatsworth, CA, and
information provided by food manufacturers.